D1432973

WALT WHITMAN

of the

New York Aurora

Walt Whitman
of the New York Aurora
EDITOR AT TWENTY-TWO

A Collection of Recently Discovered Writings
edited by

JOSEPH JAY RUBIN

CHARLES H. BROWN

GREENWOOD PRESS, PUBLISHERS
WESTPORT, CONNECTICUT

Library of Congress Cataloging in Publication Data

Whitman, Walt, 1819-1892.
    Walt Whitman of the New York Aurora.

    I. New York Aurora.   II. Title.
[PS3203.R8 1972]   818'.3'07   72-5277
ISBN 0-8371-5724-2

Originally published in 1950 by Bald Eagle Press,
State College, Pennsylvania

Reprinted with the permission of Joseph J. Rubin

Reprinted by Greenwood Press,
a division of Williamhouse-Regency Inc.

First Greenwood Reprinting 1972
Second Greenwood Reprinting 1974

Library of Congress Catalog Card Number 72-5277

ISBN 0-8371-5724-2

Printed in the United States of America

Acknowledgments

We wish to express our thanks to the Paterson (N.J.) Library for the extended use of the *AURORA* file, and to Professor William L. Werner of The Pennsylvania State College for his preface and his reading of the manuscript. Also helpful were Margaret Spangler, Professor Stanley T. Williams, the American Antiquarian Society, the Brooklyn Public Library, the Columbia University Library, the Long Island Historical Society, the New York Public Library, and The Pennsylvania State College Library.

J. J. R.
C. H. B.

Preface

I n this collection *Joseph Jay Rubin and Charles H.
Brown present an important discovery—more than
180 articles and 2 poems written by Walt Whitman for the New York AURORA which he edited in the spring
of 1842. Believed lost or destroyed these hundred years, a
single volume of this defunct daily had lain unnoticed in the
files of the Paterson (N.J.) Library until discovered by Professor Rubin;[1] none of the material has appeared in any biog-
raphy or collection of Whitman's writings. There are, of
course, a number of other valuable collections of his journalistic material:* THE GATHERING OF THE FORCES ; THE UN-
COLLECTED POETRY AND PROSE OF WALT WHITMAN ; I SIT
AND LOOK OUT ; NEW YORK DISSECTED. *But all of these
are of other periods. The AURORA discovery enables us to
examine and understand for the first time one of the starting
stretches of the poet's "long foreground."*

*Almost all these articles are unsigned, but Whitman wrote
"most of the copy" for the AURORA during his two months
of editorship and almost certainly all the editorials. Without
attempting to establish every one of these items as Whitman's,
Professors Rubin and Brown have presented abundant inter-
nal evidence of Whitman's authorship by annotating later appearances of the same material and convincing parallels in
style.*

*These editorials, timely but often unimportant in themsel-
ves, foreshadow the later, enduring writings of the poet. The
first and longest section shows his love of Manhattan, his lusty
appetite for life, his cataloguing habit, his ecstasies, and his
"laziness." The sections of political controversy are the raw*

material for DEMOCRATIC VISTAS and for the political philosophy of LEAVES OF GRASS. Of real significance is Whitman's violent participation in an issue not yet resolved in the United States: public aid for church schools. References to current news reveal his first known direct connection with Emerson, his love of Dickens' novels, his early PENCHANT *for French phrases, and his interest in theatre and opera. A final selection of sentimental reveries, like Hawthorne's or "Ik Marvel's," deals with the subjects that Whitman returned to in his later years of illness—dreams, death, and the life of the soul.*

W. L. WERNER
Professor of American Literature
THE PENNSYLVANIA STATE COLLEGE

Contents

Contents

Part II

"We never intend to mince matters---to stop for honeyed words . . ."

Contents

Part III

"Government is at best but a necessary evil."

Part IV

"In writing, it is occasionally requisite to have ideas."

Contents

Part V

"We determined to perpetrate a few paragraphs of sentiment."

Introduction

NSON HERRICK AND JOHN F. ROPES established the New York *Aurora* in November, 1841, as a twopenny daily. Since 1838 they had been publishing the *Atlas*, one of the more successful Sunday papers; possession of a prosperous weekly and an adequate printing plant gave them courage to compete with the some twenty newspapers in the city—all fighting for advertising, circulation, and political patronage.

Their motives, as they explained in their first issue, were patriotic:

> Nearly every paper in New York is wholly or in part, controlled by foreigners. Some of them are as good republicans as live—but many of them are as foreign in feeling as in birth, and most are lamentably ignorant of our country, our institutions, and our people. Some of them hate, and would do anything in their power to injure the land that gives them shelter and subsistence. The publishers of the *Aurora* are Americans. The leading editor is a Yankee from the Granite State, and, without the slightest feeling of proscription, American writers, of equal talent, will always be preferred to foreigners, simply because they understand better the genius of the people for whom they write.

Herrick and Ropes referred specifically to James Gordon Bennett, a native of Scotland, and to Park Benjamin, born in British Guiana; the *Aurora* would attack both of these men frequently and vituperatively.

The Yankee editor, Thomas Low Nichols of New Hampshire, had forsaken the study of medicine at Dartmouth for journalism. He had worked for Bennett's evening edition of the *Herald*, and his contributions, he confessed in an autobiography, were "so much in Mr. Bennett's style, in thought and expression, impudence and egotism, that my paragraphs were copied and credited to him about as often as his own."[1]

The *Aurora*, Nichols announced in his first editorial, would be politically independent, but

> democratic, in the strongest sense of the word. Whatever is contrary to Democracy, among Democratic Whigs or Democratic Republicans, will find little favor. Consequently, the party that is nearest right will fare best with us, and neither, we suspect, will consider us of much dependence as a partizan.

Not compelled to follow and promote the fortunes of a political party, the *Aurora* gave little space to correspondence from Albany and Washington; nor did it compete with other dailies in rushing European news into print. Primarily a local paper, the *Aurora* from the start devoted more columns than any other daily to the brilliant social activity of the season. Nichols printed detailed descriptions of the soirees at Charaud's and Carlton's; the entertainment at Palmo's and the Tivoli Saloon; prize fights, lectures, Fanny Ellsler's dancing in *La Sylphide;* the more sensational scandals like the trial of John Colt for murder. It was its social emphasis that caused the *Aurora* to be described as "the acknowledged journal of the beau monde, the Court Journal of our democratic aristocracy."[2]

After three months of successful editorship in which the circulation of the *Aurora* reached a respectable five thousand—surpassed by the *Sun,* the *Herald,* and Horace Greeley's new *Tribune* among the "cheap" papers and by two or three of the older sixpenny or Wall Street papers—Nichols was fired because he printed libelous charges of graft in a city pipe-laying project. He left the paper February 22, 1842.

Not until five weeks later did Herrick and Ropes announce a successor to Nichols. On March 28 they published this statement at the head of the editorial columns on the second page:

> The publishers of the Aurora would respectfully announce to their friends and the public that they have secured the services of Mr. Walter Whitman, favorably known as a bold, energetic and original writer, as their leading editor. The addition of Mr. W. to the editorial department of the Aurora, the publishers feel assured, will enable them to carry out their original design of establishing a sound, fearless and independent daily paper, which shall at all times and on all occasions advocate and sustain the dignity and interests of our country. The American public have severely felt the want of a journal which, in its sentiments and opinions, while it is biased by no undue prejudices against foreigners, will be far different from those newspapers which
> "Bend the pliant hinges of the knee,
> That thrift may follow fawning."[3]

But Whitman's association with the *Aurora* began several weeks before the March 28 announcement. As early as February 23 the *Aurora* carried the first of six articles he may have written on "Walks in Broadway." Though the pieces are unsigned, their style and tone are typically those of Whitman:

> Yesterday! What a glorious day—glorious as being our national father's birth. At meridian we took a promenade in Broadway. Every body seemed stirring and in good humor. The flags waved from the City Hall and the places of amusement, and proudly the few "revolutioners" who yet linger with us, paraded around. It is right to make something of a stir upon such

an occasion—it is right to do honor to the memory of the man
who successfully reared the standard of liberty in the world—
the thunder and lightning of whose moral and intellectual bat-
teries shivered, scathed, consumed the monuments of tyranny
which overshadowed the world.

Whitman may have started writing for the *Aurora* as one of the
paper's numerous penny-a-liners. Years later in *Specimen Days*, in
one of his rare references to his early newspaper work, Whitman
wrote: "I next went to the *Aurora* daily in New York City—a sort
of free lance."[4]

There is more conclusive evidence that Whitman was working
regularly for the *Aurora* by the beginning of the second week in
March. On March 8 the *Aurora* printed a long tribute to McDonald
Clarke, an eccentric Broadway character known as "the mad poet."
This article, one of several *Aurora* editorials which Whitman reprinted or made use of later, he incorporated in a sketch published
in the Brooklyn *Eagle* on June 13, 1846, about Clarke's burial place,
Greenwood Cemetery. Another March 8 article, "Our City," ob-
viously was the basis of one Whitman published in *Life Illustrated*
on August 9, 1856. And in a March 28 *Aurora* editorial Whitman
referred to prior service on the paper: "Some weeks or two ago, we
gave the readers of the Aurora as fair and distinct a view of 'political prospects,' in our country, as sharp eyes and attentive observation could delineate."

In the weeks of trial before March 28 Whitman proved to Herrick and Ropes that he had the ability to edit a metropolitan daily
in competition with such journalists as Bennett, Webb, Greeley,
Bryant, Beach, and Noah. Though not yet twenty-three, Whitman
had behind him ten years of experience in printshops and newspaper offices. He had been printer's devil for William Hartshorne,
master printer and foreman of the Long Island *Patriot*, and for
Alden Spooner of the Long Island *Star*. By 1836 he was a journeyman printer in New York; by 1838 he was editor-printer of his own
weekly, the *Long Islander*. A year on James J. Brenton's weekly
Democrat at Jamacia completed Whitman's Long Island stint.

His New York experience, thus far, had been brief but intense:
work at 30 Ann Street for Park Benjamin's weekly *New World*,
and by the start of 1842, the *Brother Jonathan*, another of the era's
"great beasts"—as Greeley called these huge and hurried but immensely popular literary weeklies.

The *Aurora* publishers' tribute to Whitman in the announcement
of his appointment as editor indicates their appreciation of his
other accomplishments. The year before, on July 29, 1841, Whit-

man had achieved political prominence when he addressed a giant
Democratic rally in New York. The *Evening Post* and the *New
Era* devoted more space to his remarks than to those of any of the
other speakers. Whitman could also boast of literary recognition.
He had written for the *New World* and the *Brother Jonathan,* and
most important of all for the *Democratic Review,* whose title-page
carried the names of Hawthorne, Bryant, Lowell, Whittier, Longfellow, Paulding, and Simms. As recently as March 5, 1842, the
publishers of the *Aurora* could have read praise for one of Whitman's tales. "A very neat and fanciful performance," Bryant's *Evening Post* said of the young writer's work.

The editorship his, Whitman soon discovered a deadline for a
New York daily was not to be taken as casually as that for a Long
Island weekly:

> The consciousness that several thousand people will look for
> the Aurora as regularly as for breakfasts, and that they expect
> in it an intellectual repast—something *piquant,* and something
> solid, and something sentimental and something humorous—and
> all dished up in "our own peculiar way"—this consciousness,
> we say, implies no small responsibility upon a man. Yet it is de-
> lightful. Heavy as it weighs, we have no indisposition to "take
> the responsibility."[5]

Happily, encouragement came from his friends whenever the young
editor encountered them in the city streets, hotels, and business
houses. The press also praised him:

> The Aurora.—A marked change for the better has come over
> this spirited little daily since the accession of Mr. Whitman to the
> "vacant chair." There is, nevertheless, a dash of egotism occasion-
> ally.[6]

There was, however, an occasional irritant. The young editor was
not quite so well known as he thought he should be. He had, for
example, been stopped by the doorman at a market festival and
forced "to chaffer ten minutes before admittance." Commenting
somewhat petulantly on the incident, he said: "When any one connected with the Aurora takes the trouble to visit public places—he
considers that if there is any favor in the matter, it certainly does
not come from them to him."[7]

But ordinarily nothing disturbed his feeling of importance as
editor of one of the city's leading papers. A few years before he
had been an unknown journeyman printer. The sights and sounds,
the crowds, the buildings, were just as exciting as ever, but as *the*
Mr. Whitman of the *Aurora* he could pretend an air of condescen-
sion toward it all. Dressed in his frock coat, "a grey one," wearing

a hat, "a plain, neat fashionable, black one," and bearing a cane, "a heavy, dark beautifully polished, hook ended one,"[8] he took daily strolls about the city, proud of his appearance. When he came upon a group of children playing a game on the sidewalk, he recorded the comment of one of the urchins that they would have to break the line because "there comes a gentleman." But *the* Mr. Whitman of the *Aurora* was too fine a person to break up the game. When asked to detour around the group, Whitman did so. "What wonderful powers children have of discriminating who is possessed of a courteous, kindly, manful and creditable disposition!"[9] he exclaimed.

As editor of the *Aurora*, Whitman was responsible for the content of a four-page paper of six columns 21 inches long and 2 7/16 inches wide. The first, third, and fourth pages carried advertising —small, compactly set tributes to patent medicines; notices of services for hire and goods for sale such as a "self-revolving, self-cocking pocket pistol"; an entire column "house ad" for the publications of the expanding publishing firm of Herrick, West, and Ropes, who called their plant at 162 Nassau Street the "Great American Newspaper Establishment!!" In addition to the *Aurora* and the *Atlas* ("This large and beautifully printed paper, published every Sunday morning, is devoted to literature, the fine arts, the drama, and the news of the day."), their publications now included the *Dollar Weekly* ("The Cheapest Paper in the World!!") and the Saturday *Washingtonian* ("devoted to the cause of Temperance, and to the support of the principles and doctrines of the Washingtonians").

From time to time the front page featured an illustrated article of New York types: a fireman, a butcher boy, the driver of a horsecar. Correspondence, clippings from out-of-town papers, reports of balls, and a poem or two helped fill the front page. The editor's important leaders went on the second page, together with news, reports and comment on the day's events, Washington and Albany correspondence, the police and court reports, and more lush descriptions of the New York social season. Advertisements, short clippings from other papers, and jokes filled the third and fourth pages—and supplemented the second when needed:

> The Yale Banner, a paper started by the students, and edited with great spirit, says, 'Yale has *turned out* some great men.' Pretty good for sophs.[10]

The *Aurora* staff was small. Whitman, describing his duties, told his readers that he was responsible for keeping eight or ten compositors busy and that he wrote most of the copy. Apparently there was a reporter to cover the courts and the police stations. On November 25, 1841, the *Aurora* printed this notice: "A gentleman capable of filling the situation of assistant editor of a daily paper, may find it for his advantage to apply immediately to the editor of the Aurora." David Russell Lee may have been the gentleman hired, for in noticing his resignation August 30, 1842, the *Aurora* said he had worked for the paper since its beginning and praised him as "one of the most capable, persevering and industrious reporters ever connected with the press in this city." The *Aurora* regularly bought material from contributors; penny-a-liners wrote its lengthy social accounts.

According to the standards of the day, the *Aurora* was a well printed, attractive newspaper. The nameplate across the top of the first page was in a modern Roman face. Occasionally small label headlines were used. Most of the advertising was set in agate type, and the news in nonpareil. Despite the fact that all type was handset, the *Aurora* came off the press remarkably free from typographical errors.

II

During Whitman's career as a journalist, editorship implied conflict. The quarrel in which he found himself embroiled day after day on the *Aurora* was political. His weapons were abuse, sectarianism, and even intolerance; they color unpleasantly this phase of Whitman's career. But if his editorial conduct and language cannot be admired or defended, they can be explained.

In 1840, Bishop John Hughes on behalf of the seventy thousand Roman Catholics in New York had demanded a share of public education funds for the parochial schools. The Public School Society twice rejected his demands. Anti-Catholic feeling increased in the next two years and became openly belligerent before the spring election of 1842. An astute politician, Bishop Hughes succeeded in winning Tammany support by threatening to employ the united vote of the Catholic constitutents as an opposition bloc in the New York mayoralty and aldermanic election unless the Democratic members of the New York Senate voted for the passage of a bill to allocate funds to parochial schools.

The *Aurora* watched this electioneering activity with great anxiety:

> Though professing to be by no means of excitable temperament—we are ever aroused to the utmost, by any such conduct as this of the dastardly Hughes, and his kindred fanatical demagogues. The farthest stretch of condemnation cannot go too far against any proceedings which put in jeopardy the soundness and purity of the elective franchise.[11]

Whitman, implacably opposed to anything that would destroy the traditional separation of church and state, attempted to swing Tammany to his point of view; and, as discord within Tammany became more apparent, the *Aurora*, which had hitherto professed to be politically independent, even made a bid to be designated as the Democratic party organ. Whitman's opposition to the school bill was a failure: it passed the Senate by a vote of 13 to 12, three days before the city election.

So incensed was Whitman that, despite his previous loyalty to the Democratic party, he urged his readers not to vote in the city election. That the rabble-rousing editorials Whitman had been writing for the *Aurora* echoed many voices was proved on election day. It was a day marked by riots between the Native Americans and the Irish. Whitman applauded the routing of the "bog trotters" by the Spartans, a Tammany group led by Michael Walsh and Yankee Sullivan, the prizefighter. When a mob stoned Bishop Hughes' house, Whitman mentioned the destruction with sarcastic regret: "Had it been the reverend hypocrite's head, instead of his windows, we would hardly find it in our soul to be sorrowful."[12]

The election was a draw between the Democrats and the Whigs. The Democrats elected the mayor, but the Whigs succeeded in naming a majority of the members of the Common Council. Whitman wrote: "We were never brought up to rejoice at the defeat of Democratic candidates. Yet our republican schooling has taught us that there are duties far higher and holier than devotion to local interests of party."[13]

The resistance offered by the *Aurora* to the entrance of the Roman Catholic church into secular education and party politics parallels the action of the anti-Catholic group known as the Native Americans. One contemporary accused the *Aurora* of being a Native American publication; another invited the paper to join in spreading such Nativist doctrines as the disenfranchisement of the foreign-born and the exclusion of Catholics from office. In several editorials Whitman repudiated the accusation and rejected the invitation.

There is no reason to doubt Whitman's sincerity in repudiating the Native American invitation. He might have found it politically wise and financially profitable to join a party which had been growing in numbers and importance since 1834. By 1844 the Nativists would have enough strength to elect as mayor of New York the publisher whom Whitman admired, James Harper. The names of Harper, S. F. Morse, and Seba Smith, the Nativist leaders, indicate the respectability of the anti-Catholic movement.

The political philosophy motivating Whitman's attack upon Bishop Hughes was not Nativism but Jeffersonianism. Whitman, like Jefferson whom he quoted, believed in "the absolute and lasting severance of the church from the state."[14]

> As Americans we shall ever oppose religious politics, be they introduced by Episcopalian, Presbyterian, Baptist, Methodist or Catholic . . . We go for the letter of the Constitution.[15]

The young editor had come of age in a decade dominated by Jeffersonian anti-clericalism; his other major political deities—Jackson and Van Buren—and many minor ones had also made perfectly clear their belief in the wisdom of keeping church and state separate.

This controversy left Whitman with one residue of positive value. Some of his *Aurora* editorials show that he considered it equally vital to war against the encroachment of certain kinds of European literature, "a literature which, being under the patronage of courts and princes and haughty church, is not fitted for our beloved America."[16]

III

Despite Bishop Hughes, rival editors, and inexorable deadlines, Whitman found time to sample and enjoy New York. He chose a quiet, clean boarding house—so genteel that the proprietor's name was displayed on the door in a neat brass plaque, without a vulgar "boarding" sign. At Mrs. Chipman's, Whitman enjoyed both pleasant company and good food. He became convinced of the comfort of his quarters when, after being locked out accidentally, he had to spend the night at lodgings chosen hurriedly: he lay awake until morning listening to a quartet of snorers.

The city, "a mighty world in itself,"[17] absorbed the young editor. He seemed willing to walk the streets at all hours in search of different experiences. He would start from the *Aurora* office, only four doors from City Hall, "with its redundance of marble tracery and ornament." Then, pass Tammany Hall on his way to the fashionable

trottoir, Broadway. He could view that "most villainous specimen of
architecture," the Park theater; St. Paul's "which, with its steeple
the other way, seems as if it wanted to walk off from amid so much
tumult and din"; the windows of Colman's book store; Trinity
Church; the Astor House. He then would join the glittering promenade of fashionable people all heading for the Battery and then
he would write ecstatically:

> Gods! what a glorious morning it was! Just enough of ener-
> vating, voluptuous heat—and just enough breeze to fill the wings
> of the zephyrs—and just enough sunshine to reflect a sparkle
> in the eyes of beautiful women—and just enough people walking
> on the pave to make one continued, ceaseless, devilish, provoking,
> delicious, glorious jam![18]

Varying his pleasure, he visited a gymnasium and pistol gallery;
spent an afternoon at the Battery listening to the "sublime tone"
of the ocean or watching two steamers race; visited the American
Museum where a Gypsy girl read his palm. Evening might include
the spectacle of a fire, a temperance lecture, a flower show. Leaving
the office late at night, he observed the Aurora Borealis: "It did
not shoot up in columns, as it usually does, but rolled up in waves,
like an illuminated ocean."[19] Even then a caresser of life, he wrote
about his experiences, though apologizing that as a busy editor he
really should "dash into" a political or a journalistic foe.[20]

Though his editorial work would not allow time off for complete
indulgence, the theatre continued to exercise the allure of his adol-
escent days. Programs were a mingling of the trivial, the shoddy,
the spectacular, and the enduring. At the Park, Bouccicault was the
new dramatist; Shakespeare still held the stage occasionally at the
Chatham. J. R. Scott played *Macbeth* and *Coriolanus;* John Sefton,
the *Golden Farmer;* T. D. Rice, his famous Jim Crow and Jumbo
Jim. A lover of music, too, Whitman heard the opera *Norma* and
Alpine melodies sung by the Rainers.

Whitman announced editorially his support for building an American drama, and he watched with admiration Charlotte Cushman's efforts to create a national theatre. When he was invited to
participate, he answered: "Let us have an international copyright
law, and we shall have a national drama, and literature also."[21]

Whitman's other literary interests reveal themselves through occasional comment. In a defense of Dickens, he pointed out to *Aurora*
readers that Boz had not exaggerated the wickedness of his characters, for were not James Gordon Bennett and Park Benjamin like
Quilp, Sikes, and Fagin? Whitman attacked other popular English
writers: the "flippant perpetrators" of *Charles O'Malley, The Irish*

Dragoon, Random Recollections in Exeter Hall, and *Handy Andy.*
In scattered paragraphs he scolded Cooper for his libel suits against
editors, praised Longfellow as being "one of the best of American
bards,"[22] and sneered at the poetic and dramatic pretensions of
Park Benjamin. He declared that Bryant was the greatest poet of
the day. Late in April Whitman announced a plan to write a weekly
literary criticism, but he left the paper before executing it.

The most important intellectual contribution that the city may
have made to Whitman during his *Aurora* career was a first-hand
acquaintance with Emerson and transcendentalism. He had had several opportunities to learn something about Emerson: the *Democratic Review* had carried an extensive review of *Nature;* the *New
World* had examined the *Essays;* and the *Tribune* had reprinted
them. As early as February 28, 1842, the *Aurora* had carried a column definition of transcendentalism. And now, early in March,
Emerson came to the New York Society Library to read a series of
six lectures on "The Times."

On Monday, March 7, the *Aurora* described Emerson's Saturday
evening lecture on "Poetry of the Times." On Tuesday, the *Aurora*
tried to explain transcendentalism, sketching in four hundred words
its Kantian basis and Emerson's interpretation: "In the language of
Mr. Emerson himself—'This is the era of individuality. It is All
Souls Day.'" On March 15, the *Aurora* described Emerson:

> The lecture of this great gun of transcendentalism was at-
> tended by a very full and fashionable audience last evening.
> Mr. E. is a quiet, easy speaker, with much grace, and a little of
> the Yankee twang in his voice. We should not be surprised if he
> made a good many converts in Gotham.

Two weeks later Whitman noted that Emerson's lectures had given
a "severe shock to the religious mind of the community."[23]

Whitman again expressed a Jeffersonian concept, that "the best
government is that which governs least," when he recommended
fewer sessions of legislatures and Congress; as a result of their
work, he said, things were always worse at the end of a session than
at the beginning. He condemned the "officiousness of the law-making
powers" and their tendency to "meddle with every thing, and derange every thing—from our intercourse with foreign empires down
to the oyster trade."[24] He struck out boldly against a proposed bill
to make licentiousness and immorality a penal offense. Laws would
not, could not remake man nor "supersede nature." His editorial
contained this statement of his faith in the individual:

> We are beginning to feel, not in theory merely, (that has
> long been the case), but in reality, that every being with a

rational soul is an *independent man*, and that one is such a man as another, and that all sovereign rights reside within himself, and that it is a dangerous thing to delegate them to legislatures.[26]

Whitman printed two of his own poems in the *Aurora*. "The Death and Burial of McDonald Clarke. A Parody" is based upon Charles Wolfe's "The Burial of Sir John Moore at Corunna," an extremely popular period piece. His other poem, "Time to Come," is a revision of "Our Future Lot," printed first in his own *Long Islander*. These derivatory juvenilia merely accentuate the precocity of Whitman's other achievements.

Whitman's *Aurora* prose reveals more of his native character— his individuality or eccentricity of style, his intuitive rather than logical presentation of thought, his broadly impressionistic reception of facts and ideas, his sentimentality. He admitted later that his poetic method was "to write in the gush, the throb, the flood of the moment."[26] The habit may have derived from the need to write under pressure to meet newspaper deadlines. Some of his early prose mannerisms would be carried over into his later poetry: his ejaculatory style, his long catalogues, his ignoring of conventional syntax, and the use of the dash.

Not all of the levels of prose language in the *Aurora* are equally effective. Whitman was quick to identify a rival's errors: Of James Gordon Bennett, he wrote, "Yesterday he came out with one of his usual ungrammatical leaders in which *shall* and *will* were most beautifully confounded." But he himself could write of the Globe Hotel as "a tasty structure," and use a "pretty considerable" number; or flavor his editorials with "soft soap," "whole hog Irish," and "we do not expect to set the North River on fire." He could not resist using this one twice: "General Scott knocked all his prospects into a disarranged chapeau."

But the young editor's most surprising stylistic trait is his use of French words and phrases. Six years before he would hear French spoken in New Orleans, Whitman wrote of young inmates of a detention home lining up "en militaire" and marching to the "salle et manager [*sic*]." In another article he used "nous verrons." Whitman probably picked up his borrowings from the *Aurora's* society reports, for French phrases were used frequently to give *ton* to these accounts.

IV

For almost two months Whitman had written of himself and of New York: of politics, personalities, dreams, curiosities, ideas. He had displayed utter hostility toward religious interference in secular affairs; he had waged the usual editorial warfare with several contemporaries. He had exhibited eagerness to mingle with the life of the city and assimilate all of its strange and various incidents—murder trials, dances, auctions, the theatre, Emersonian transcendentalism, gossip about Daniel Webster's morals. Proud and handsome in his finery and happy in the glow of youth, Whitman had walked the streets:

> Wasn't it brave! And didn't we laugh (not outwardly—that would have been vulgar; but in the inward soul's bedchamber) with very excess of delight and gladness? O, it is a beautiful world we live in, after all![27]

The one other thing Whitman did ended his editorship: he quarreled with his employers. On May 3, the *Aurora* printed a squib, "There is a man about our office so lazy that it takes two men to open his jaws when he speaks. If you kick him he's too idle to cry, for then he'd have to wipe his eyes. *What* can be done with him?" On May 16 the *Aurora* carried this announcement under the masthead: "Mr. Walter Whitman desires us to state that he has been for three or four weeks past, and now is, entirely disconnected with the editorial department of the Aurora."

According to William Cauldwell, a young typesetter in the *Aurora* shop, the quarrel came over Whitman's refusal to allow Herrick to "tone" the leaders. "If you want such stuff in the *Aurora*, write it yourself," he told his publisher. Herrick countered by calling Whitman "the laziest fellow who ever undertook to edit a city paper."[28]

Whitman's revenge came that summer when he used space in his next paper, the *Evening Tattler*, to repeat insulting tirades against Herrick and Ropes written by the editor of the Hartford (Connecticut) *Review*. The *Aurora* publishers claimed that the Hartford editor owed them seventy dollars for the sale of woodcuts and called him "a contemptible sponge." Whitman gleefully followed the fight and brought to the New York public the latest exchange of insults. On August 29 Herrick and Ropes told their readers that an abusive article from the Hartford paper had appeared in "a small, 'obscure daily' now under the control of a 'pretty pup' once in our employment; but whose indolence, incompetence, loaferism and blackguard habits forced us to kick him out of office." The pretty pup, of course, was Whitman.

Herrick and Ropes quoted Whitman's own reasons for leaving the *Aurora:*

> There is in this city a trashy, scurrilous, and obscene daily paper, under charge of two as dirty fellows, as ever were able by the force of brass, ignorance of their own ignorance, and a coarse manner of familiarity, to push themselves among gentlemen. Not capable in their own sconces of constructing two lines of grammar or meaning, they are in the habit, every month or so, (for no man can remain longer than that time in their concern,) of engaging some literary person to "do" their paper. *We*—ill-starred by Fate—were, some six months since, unfortunate enough to allow ourself to be induced by the scamps in question, to take the editorial charge of their sheet. During the few weeks we continued there, we saw, in the instance of these two ill bred vagabonds, more mean selfishness—more disregard of all manliness and good manners—more low deceits—more attempts at levying "black mail"—heard more gross blasphemy and prurient conversation, than ever before in our life.

Herrick and Ropes refuted their erstwhile editor:

> This fellow tells his own story. We were fine fellows as long as we consented to pay him for loafing about our office; but we didn't happen to want him, and, 'of course' we are 'dirty fellows.'

This is the last mention of Whitman in the columns of the *Aurora.*

[The editors have reproduced the *Aurora's* exact text. Their only liberty has been taken in providing titles for some of Whitman's editorials; these insertions are enclosed with brackets.]

"New York

    is a great place

      . . . .

a mighty world

      in itself"

READER, LOOK AT HIM!

(See page 47.)

Part One

EW YORK is a great place — a mighty world in itself. Strangers who come here for the first time in their lives, spend week after week, and yet find that there are still hundreds of wonders and surprises, and (to them) oddities, which they have not had a chance of examining. Here are people of all classes and stages of rank—from all countries on the globe—engaged in all the varieties of avocations—of every grade, every hue of ignorance and learning, morality and vice, wealth and want, fashion and coarseness, breeding and brutality, elevation and degradation, impudence and modesty.

Coming up Broadway, from the Bowling Green, an observer will notice, on each side, tall, quiet looking houses, with no great aspect of life or business. These are mostly boarding houses; and notwithstanding their still look, they no doubt contain within their walls no small number of occupants. Here the sidewalks and the street present but few passengers. After passing Trinity Church, however, the crowd thickens, and the ground stories of the buildings are principally occupied as shops. Along this section of Broadway are several crack hotels. If you pass at the latter part of the day, you will see little groups of well dressed men, picking their teeth lazily, and enjoying an after dinner lounge. Near here, there are two shops which deserve especial notice. Judging by their capacious windows, they are for the sale of knicknacks, and fancy articles of all descriptions, from a chess board or an escritoire to a toothpick. From a glance at these treasures, a person can hardly help reflecting how many thousand wants, altogether imaginary, one may be led to have through the refinements of civilization.

Directly afterward, you will notice two crowds gazing at the prints in the windows of a book store. This is Colman's. If you chance to stop there for the same purpose as the rest, look out for the contents of your pockets. We mean this in a double sense; for if you are not incited to purchase some of the alluring literary beauties to be had at Colman's, it is quite possible that you may be otherwise relieved of your cash by some of the swells who there do congregate.

Then you come to where the Park thrusts out as a kind of wedge between Broadway and the beginning of Park Row. If you take the left, you have to make way against a great current of fashion, idleness, and foppery. Suppose you turn to the right.

Down you walk—first stopping to gaze a moment at St. Paul's, which, with its steeple the other way, seems as if it wanted to walk off from amid so much tumult and din—and at that very respectable small city, the Astor House. A few rods, and you are in front of an ambiguous structure, of a dirty white color, and which you internally set down in your mind as the most villainous specimen of architecture you ever beheld. This is the Park theatre—or, as some of our people, with a very untasty habit of copying whatever is foreign, term it, the Old Drury. You will not wonder, when you hear that the manager has been very unsuccessful of late, maugre all his energetic and liberal catering. What benignant spirit could ever plume his wings on the top of *such* a temple?

By and by, you arrive at an open space, whereabout, if you look sharp, you will behold the name of one of the wonders of the city —that is, the "New York Aurora."[2] In all probability your ears will be greeted with the discordant notes of the newsboys, who generally muster here in great force. A door or two further is Tammany Hall, the Mecca of democracy—the time honored, soul endeared holy of holies, to all who go for anti monopoly, and the largest freedom of the largest number.

The City Hall on the left, with its redundance of marble tracery and ornament, will not probably strike you as being anything very extensive—so pass we on.

Now you come into the region of Jews, jewelry, and second hand clothing. Here and there, the magic "three balls" hold out hope to those whose ill luck makes them grasp at even the smallest favors.

Passing the Pearl street crossing, and the Chatham theatre, you are in the large triangle which people call Chatham *square.* In the middle are dray carts, coaches, and cabs: on the right loom up small hills of furniture, of every quality, with here and there an auctioneer, standing on a table or barrel top, and crying out to the crowd around him, the merits of the articles, and the bids made for them.

Then up the Bowery, which presents the most heterogeneous melange of any street in the city: stores of all kinds and people of all kinds, are to be met with every forty rods. You come by and by to the Bowery theatre; this is one of the best looking buildings in the city.

If you keep up the Bowery, you will lose yourself at last in the midst of vacant squares, unfenced lots, and unbuilt streets.

If you turn to the right, you will come into some of the dirtiest

looking places in New York. Pitt, Ridge, Attorney and Willett
streets, and all thereabout, are quite thickly settled with German
emigrants.

If you wind your steps leftward, you will have a chance of promenading to suit any taste you may be possessed of. You can lead off
into some of the most aristocratic thorough-fares, or some of the
lowest, or some of a medium between both.

[MARCH 8, 1842]

LIFE IN NEW YORK

Whoever does not know that "our city" is the great place of the
western continent, the heart, the brain, the focus, the main spring,
the pinnacle, the extremity, the no more beyond, of the New World
—whoever does not know this, we say, must have been brought up
in a place where they "didn't take the papers," and where the
Aurora, in particular, had never scattered its effulgent light.

The two great channels of communication through the city, are
Broadway, and Chatham street, of which the Bowery is nothing
more than a continuation. At a little before sunrise, if you are an
early riser, you may behold a slight human stream, beginning to
set down Broadway. The milkmen's carts, and occasionally a car-
riage from one of the landings where steamboats arrive early in
the morning, dash hastily along the street. The pedestrians are
nearly all workmen, going to their daily toil, and most of them carrying little tin kettles containing their dinner; newsmen, also, with
bundles of the damp morning papers strapped to their sides; people
now and then, of more fashionable appearance, who have wisely
roused themselves from torpid slumber, and come forth to snuff the
morning air. Frequently, too, you may meet a sleepy looking boy,
neatly dressed, and swinging a large brass key as he goes along. He
is an under clerk in some store, and on his way to open the establishment, sweep it out, and, if need may be, kindle the fire. Be careful, as you pass, lest you get a sousing from some of those Irish
servant women, scrubbing the marble stoops, and dashing pails of
water upon the flagging of the side walks.

As the sun mounts the horizon, the scene assumes another and a
far different aspect. Gradually the working-day appearance of Broadway is changed, and the patricians of our great metropolis take possession in force. On the sunny side as the noon draws on, beautiful
women and good looking men, occasionally interspersed with an

over-dressed dandy, meet the eye. It may well be said, indeed, that in America there is only *the* Broadway.

If you have travelled over the world, you will hardly remember a livelier or more brilliant and dashy scene, than the pave presents in Broadway from two till four o'clock in the afternoon of a pleasant day.

At sunset, the direction of the current is contrary to what it was in the morning—setting upward, that is, from the Bowling Green to Union Park. The same people who went down in the morning now return, carrying with them the same little tin kettles. But the crowd is at this time so much greater that the infusion of the home-ward bound men is but a drop in the bucket.

[MARCH 14, 1842]

LIFE IN A NEW YORK MARKET

One Saturday night, not long since, a fantasy popped into our brain that we would like to take a stroll of observation through *a market*. Accordingly, sallying forth, we proceeded to put our wishes into execution. A short distance brought us to that large, dirty look-ing structure in Grand street, where much store of meats, vegetables, et cetera, is daily dispensed to the sojourners of that section of our city.

We entered. What an array of rich, red sirloins, luscious steaks, delicate and tender joints, muttons, livers, and all the long list of various flesh stuffs, burst upon our eyes! There they hung, tempting, seductive—capable of begetting ecstacies in the mouth of an epi-cure—or curses in the throat of a Grahamite.[3] By the powers of cookery! the condition of the republic is not so grievous after all; we cannot be on the verge of despair, when such spectacles as these may be witnessed in the land!

How the crowd rolls along! There comes a journeyman mason (we know him by his *limy* dress) and his wife—she bearing a little white basket on her arm. With what an independent air the mason looks around upon the fleshy wares; the secret of the matter is, that he has his past week's wages in his pocket, and therefore puts he on that devil-may-care countenance. So marvellous an influence hath money in making a man feel valiant and as good as his neighbor.

Notice that prim, red cheeked damsel, for whom is being weighed a small pork steak. She is maid of all work to an elderly couple, who have sent her to purvey for their morrow's dinner. How the young fellow who serves her, at the same time casts saucy, lovable glances at her pretty face; and she is nothing loth, but pleased enough at the chance of a little coquetry. Cunning minx! she but carries out the foible of her sex, and apes her superiors.

With slow and languid steps moves along a white faced, thin bodied, sickly looking, middle aged man. He is dressed in a shabby suit, and no doubt will look long and watchfully before he spends the two ten cent pieces to which his outlay is limited. Poor fellow! he is evidently a member of one of those trades which require a man to stay cooped up in the house in some constrained bodily position. The healthy air, and the pleasant sunshine, and the delicious influences of the outer world, have not been showered upon him; and here he is, fast sinking into the grave. What a mockery of the benefits of civilization!

That fat, jolly featured woman, is the keeper of a boarding house for mechanics, and every one else who chooses to take up with good solid accommodations, for a moderate price. She is foraging for her Sunday dinner. What is it to be? She has piece after piece taken down from its hook, but none seem to suit her. She passes on.

A heterogeneous mass, indeed, are they who compose the bustling crowd that fills up the passage way. Widows with sons, boys of twelve or fourteen, to walk with them for company; wives, whose husbands are left at home to "take care of the children"; servant women; cooks; old maids (these are the especial horror of every salesman in the market;) careful housewives of grades high and low; men with the look of a foreign clime; all sorts and sizes, kinds, ages, and descriptions, all wending, and pricing, and examining, and purchasing.

But those butchers! what jovial dogs they are! Notice with what easy impudence they accost every passer by, and how they swear by all that's sacred, that on *their* stall may be found exactly what the said passer by desires to purchase. With sleeves rolled up, and one corner of their white apron tucked under the waist string—to whoever casts an enquiring glance at their stand, they gesticulate with the grace, the affected bendings and twistings of a French dancing master. Neither does rebuff discourage them. With amusing perseverance, they play off on every new passenger the same lures and the same artifice that have been tried and failed in so many previous cases. And when they have nothing else to do, they amuse themselves with a jig, or a break down. The capacities of the "market roarers" in all the mystery of a double shuffle, it needs not our word to endorse.[4] And the whistling!—the butcher boy's whistling! whose ear has not drunk in the full, rich melody thereof?

Perhaps, search the whole land through, you will not find a hand-
somer, more manly looking set of men than our butchers. They may
be known by their clear complexions, healthy look, bright eyes—
and by their saucy good nature, their bull dog courage, their im-
pudent wit, their hankering for a frequent "muss," and their disposition to rows and fights generally.

Walking along to another section of the place—we are in the
region of vegetable stands, huckster women, and poultry sellers.
Near by, is a coffee and cake stall. Every now and then a hungry
boy, or a man whose pressure of business has caused him to go
without his supper, or some one else, tempted by the savory fumes
of the coffee and the rich "kraulers," seats himself or herself, and
commences murderous attacks upon the good things of the fair
maid officiating behind the counter. Within three yards, notice those
two urchins eyeing the "kraulers" with envious eyes; let us open
the flood gates of our charity, and give the youngsters a half dime,
that they may revel in the tid bits that have evidently so taken their
fancy. There! the fashionable may laugh our notions to scorn—but
we feel more satisfaction from having bestowed on those awkward
boys a ten minutes' joy, than if we had received sunny greetings
from the proudest belle in Broadway, or heard that "our party"
had gained the gubernatorial contest.

Such are some of the scenes of "life in a New York market." It
would be no loss for a man who loves to see the workings of human
nature—the uncouth, natural outpourings of the feelings of the
heart—to take a stroll, now and then, in the mazes of these minia-
ture worlds. Lessons may be learnt there, and pictures of life seen
there, which the gilded halls of rank, and the refined circles of the
town, with all their boasted privileges, cannot confer.

[MARCH 16, 1842]

NEW YORK BOARDING HOUSES[5]

English travellers sometimes characterise the Americans as a
"trading, swapping, spitting race."[6] Others again consider our most
strongly marked features to be inquisitiveness, public vain glory,
and love of dollars. If *we* were called upon to describe the universal
Yankee nation in laconic terms, we should say, they are "a boarding
people." Perhaps the appellation will more particularly apply to
the New Yorkers, and denizens of two or three other large cities;

but it holds good, to a certain degree, for every section of the republic.

It will perhaps surprise many persons to hear, but it is no less true, that half the inhabitants of the city hire accommodations at these houses. Married men and single men; old women and pretty girls; milliners and masons; cobblers, colonels, and counter jumpers; tailors and teachers; lieutenants, loafers, ladies, lackbrains, and lawyers; printers and parsons—"black spirits and white, blue spirits and gray"—all "go out to board."

The New York boarding houses are of various grades—from the lordly Astor to the grub cellars near the North river docks. In Bond street, and in parts of Broadway there are the best of them— quiet, genteel, well ordered places—where people of refinement and breeding can pass their time almost as pleasantly as in a private parlor. Scattered over the city in all directions are boarding houses of a different grade—some of them perhaps as well ordered—but mostly less exclusive.

The better houses seldom have "boarding" displayed on the door, but generally the name of the proprietor, as "Mrs. C......."[7] Of course, in an establishment of this sort, conducted on any thing like "a scale," many amusing and rare specimens of human kind may be met with. Suppose, for the entertainment of the Aurora readers, we give, at a venture, descriptions of the inmates of a New York boarding house of the better order.

It is breakfast time. That fleshy, red cheeked, good looking woman at the head of the table, is the landlady. She officiates at the coffee and tea urns, and, as each person appears to be prepared for a further supply of the good things spread out so liberally there, she sees that his wants are attended to.

Mr. K., the gentleman at the corner, is a good humored New Englander, and Mr. D., next to him, is from the same section of our country. W. is a dry goods keeper in Greenwich street, and H. an elderly bachelor who has a clothing store down town. A. is a Jewish gentleman of Chatham street, S. one of a well known publishing firm in this city, and the next two young fellows are clerks in Broadway. Mr. B., at the lower head of the table, is a jeweller and a gentleman; Y. is from Saratoga Springs; N., a salesman in a shop near by; Dr. H., a dentist and physician; Mrs. H., his wife; an elderly woman, the mother of the landlady; and several others, ladies, &c., whom we feel delicate about mentioning.

Here you have a fair specimen of the New York boarding house, selected at random; it is done merely for the purpose of giving the uninitiated reader an idea of the company to be met with there.

The rate of remuneration in these places, is from three dollars to six, and sometimes higher. In mechanics' boarding houses, the customary price is somewhat less than three dollars. In our rough and tumble through the world, we have taken up quarters in all the various kinds, and therefore "speak from experience."

[MARCH 18, 1842]

THE LAST OF LIVELY FRANK[8]

One of the pleasantest afternoons of last week, as we were taking a stroll on the Battery, a man came up and accosted us by name, asking if we had an hour's leisure to accompany him to the upper part of the city. A second look at the stranger brought him to our recollection as one whom we had met in other scenes and other places. He stated to us the object for which he desired our visit, and we readily accompanied him.

Passing up the walks of the beautiful promenade which is the pride of Gotham, we made our egress through the iron gate, and wended along Broadway, the Park, Chatham street, and Bowery, to Grand street. Here our conductor turned to the right, and after keeping on a few blocks, wheeled again to the left, and led us down one of those dirty narrow thoroughfares, which abound in that section of the city. He stopped in front of a blackish, grimy, miserable looking house, and opening the door without knocking, bade us enter with him. Not riskless of some danger of barked shins or a bruised head, we followed our guide up a filthy stairs and into an attic room.

Though by the statements our acquaintance had made in the beginning, we expected to witness bleak poverty and the worst traits of destitution, we were sickened and shocked by the sight that met our eyes. Upon a thing, which, for want of some other name, we suppose must be called a bed, there lay a human form. It was one that we had known in by gone times—as a fine, handsome, talented young man. Now his ghastly features, and the surrounding circumstances of penury, told a tale of chances thrown away, industry contemned, extravagance indulged in, and utter desperation at last, which it was terrible to think of.

We had known that sick man in his earlier youth. From his good temper, his vivacity, and his exuberance of animal spirits, his common appellation, among his intimate friends, was "Lively Frank." He was left an orphan in early life; but his personal attractions and his extraordinary intelligence raised him up many friends. Though this seemed a happy stroke of good luck, it proved, in the end, to be Frank's ruin. If fortune came thus uncalled, he deemed her favors trifling, and hardly worth the striving for. We have observed the same thing in many similar cases.

It would be a painful story to tell—of his negligence, his idleness, his letting his talents run to waste, and, at last, his reduction to the state in which we found him.

The poor fellow was hardly able to articulate his thanks to us for our kindness in remembering him. All his summer friends, as poverty advanced, had dropped off. Though habituated to the customs and ministerings of a gentleman, the wretched young man had for weeks languished as we now beheld him, amid the utmost coarseness and the depth of vulgar life.

He knew that he was to die. And many bitter and fearful things he said about mankind and the world, which we will not repeat. His cup was full and running over; no doubt his maledictions and harsh words were forgiven by the spirit that keeps record in heaven's chancery.

What we could do for him we did. As we came forth from the house, we very naturally thought of the similar events that are daily going on in this great city. If some potent magician could lift the veil which shrouds, in alleys, dark streets, garrets, and a thousand other habitations of want, the miseries that are every day going on among us—how would the spectacle distress and terrify the beholder! Delicate women would be seen, working themselves even to illness, that those dependent on them might not suffer; young boys forced by the circumstances wherein they are bred, to be familiar with vice and all iniquity; girls, whom absolute starvation drives at length to ruin, worse than starvation; men, of hope bereft, and almost ready to meet death with a welcome—all this would be laid bare, and be not a tenth of the horrors still left undescribed. O, what curses from desperate guilt—what chuckling from the successful rogue—what death beds unattended by the hand of succor— what groans from sick children, sounding out at midnight—what complaints of poverty and hunger, unheeded by those whose most worthless trinket would yield all the desired assistance—what lording it by brave wickedness, and crushing down of humble virtue— are ever and ever present in this mighty emporium of our modern world!

In all likelihood, before these lines meet your eyes, reader, the last pulse has throbbed, and the last breath sped, from the haples creature whose fortunes have been the text of this article.

[MARCH 21, 1842]

AN HOUR IN A BALCONY

Though during yesterday and the preceding night our city had a short touch of the quality of winter—every man, woman, and child in New York must recollect that for several days previous the weather was of the mildest, most summerlike description. On an afternoon of one of those pleasant days, as we sauntered out of the west gate of the Park, feeling in an observative mood, we recollected an old custom of ours, long since disused—we went up the stairs of the American Museum, entered the first room, took a chair, placed it in a roomy niche made by the settling in one of the front windows —and in that chair ensconced we ourself. Out before us was the busiest spectacle this busy city may present. One mighty rush of men, business, carts, carriages, and clang.

How true it is, what travellers say about our population always being in a hurry. With what restless and feverish steps they move along! It seems as though each knew his appointed time, and was determined to make the most of it. Let us pass a few remarks upon the scenes and the people that may be beheld from that balcony window.

The noisiest things which attract attention in that part of Broadway, are the omnibusses. Rumbling and bouncing along, they come, now and then stopping as some person on the sidewalk holds up his finger—a signal that he wants to take passage. The omnibus drivers are a unique race. Winter and summer, rain or shine, there they are, perched up on the tops of their vehicles, and driving ahead just the same. What a life! over the same track, and along the same street, hour after hour, and day after day. Moving and changing as is the scene, can it be otherwise than monotonous to them?[9]

A group of fashionable ladies next attracts our eyes. What splendid creatures they are—even amid the tinsel and distortion of milliners and dressmakers. After all, say what poets and rural lovers may—there is something about a polished, splendidly dressed, graceful and dashy city lady, that eclipses all else of the sex! There; we have come to a conclusion on that point.

Notice those carriages, with liveried servants. Such sights are particularly pleasing to plain republican eyes. In this imitative style, the gentleman rolls along Broadway, pompous as a militia colonel on review day—no matter if his hands be a little soiled by the measuring of broadcloth, or his clothing still retain the scent of the sugar box, the tobacco keg, the rappee[10] pot, rum cask, or even, what is worse than all, the scent of Wall street verdigris—no matter, we say; for the glory of the style aristocratic so mystifies the sense of the democratic plodders on the way side, that they can only wonder and adore.

But what objection can there be to this kind of "showing off?" Not the slightest. It indicates a great mind, a laudable ambition, an ambition to make a show in the world—and though it is merely a puppet show, it is the sort most pleasing to children and fools; and such people are the only ones whom men of sense should attempt to interest or improve. Sir Isaac Newton had not half the judgment that the countryman had who continually rang a hand bell as he passed in the streets, saying that he was determined to make some noise in the world. These worthies possess just as much sense as the countryman, only they do not show it in quite so harmless a way.

And we further contend that our Broadway aristocrats do good in the community. Laughing is an agreeable and a healthy exercise.

But it is no joke, after-all. These gentry discover their consummate folly in this sort of aping of the customs of Europe. We have no aristocracy in this country; but these poor, deluded people think that by wrapping themselves in the cloak of the true aristocrat they will be able to pass for genuine. They should remember the ass in the lion's skin. Where are their manners, their long lines of "illustrious predecessors," their identity with the government itself, their rights, titles and treasures which the wind of popular caprice cannot waft to the hand of another?

But our republican aristocrats! What are they? They are those whose brains would be more likely to breed grasshoppers than ideas —whose pedigrees should be sought for in the tinker's shop. But it may be asked, do they not do good, by scattering thus broadcast, the money which, in early life, they wrought hard and lived frugally to amass? No. A good many worthy arguers have split upon this rock. The lavish expenditure of money is not doing good unless it be spent for proper objects.

As our cogitations have already extended to a "pretty considerable" length, we shall give the remainder of them at some future time.

[MARCH 23, 1842]

THE CLERK FROM THE COUNTRY[11]

As may be well imagined, the keepers of our New York boarding houses are very frequently imposed upon. They sometimes get swindled out of large amounts—through the adroitness and cunning of the more accomplished swells. An incident came to our knowledge a few days ago, which it may not be unprofitable to lay before our readers.

In one of the most fashionable boarding houses just north of the City Hall, there applied for entertainment, one day two or three weeks since, a genteel, handsome young man, whose face seemed to carry a letter of recommendation. The landlady cheerfully and with great satisfaction admitted him as an inmate of her establishment. His occupation, he stated, was as clerk in the store of a certain well known chemist and apothecary in Broadway.

For a week, things went on very pleasantly. The young man seemed to have a great deal of leisure, and occasionally stayed out late at night. But the lady mistress, thinking it no business of hers, troubled not herself upon the subject.

All the boarders were pleased with the new comer. He was modest and polite in his deportment, and his youth, delicacy, and good looks, made him a special favorite with the ladies.

One morning after breakfast the landlady left upon a table in her room, on the second story of the house, a valuable gold watch. She was for some time busied down stairs; and while thus busied, the youth lately admitted to the house came in the front door, and went up stairs. After remaining some fifteen minutes he came down again, and left the place. In the course of the morning, the lady, having occasion to use her watch, went up to take it from the place where she had left it. It was not there. Thinking that possibly her son might have taken it with him down town, she gave herself no further trouble; until at dinner in the afternoon she found that her supposition was incorrect. The son had not seen or touched the watch.

Dinner passed away, and the young man did not return. Reluctantly, and remembering that he had been seen coming down immediately previous to the discovery of the loss, she was led to suspect him as having stolen the article missed.

The lady was grieved, perhaps, quite as much at thought of the youngster's wickedness, as of her own loss. She determined, if possible, to arrange the matter without inflicting on the youth, (if he should really prove to be guilty,) the penalty of any verdict of the law.

At supper, the young man came in. When the meal was concluded, and he took his departure from the room, the landlady stopped him as he stood in the hall with his hat in his hand—asking him to step with her for a moment into a side room.

He did so, trembling, and his lip evidently quivering. The lady saw that her suspicions were correct. She told him gently, but decidedly, what her accusation was. Tears started into the youth's eyes, and he confessed its truth. The watch, he said, after being purloined, had been placed by him into the hands of a man, an intimate acquaintance, who received from him *such* things. Street and number were given by the terrified creature—who shook like one with an ague.

Upon enquiry, and further investigation, the lady found that this youth was the son of a very respectable and wealthy farmer in a western county of New York. He had been fitted out from home— his parents no doubt under the influence of that mischievous idea which makes country people think it better for their sons to be counter jumpers than American farmers.

He had come to New York, without a home, and ignorant of all the arts and tricks of city life. His pockets being pretty liberally supplied with money, a clique of designing sharpers had got him in their toils, and made him a mere catspaw to further their schemes of villainy. Some time before, he had left his situation as clerk at the chemist's store, and his only means of paying his way, was by the funds which his new acquaintances gave him.

It was shocking to hear him tell of the lures they had used to entangle him—and how he had been led to do vicious and dangerous things for them.

The landlady immediately prepared to go, though it was evening, to the place he mentioned as the one where he had left the watch. At first, the youth demurred; but she was not to be refused.

They went. Upon knocking at the door, it was, after a few moments, opened by a coarse looking fellow, in whose presence the lady asked the youth if the person he had alluded to was the one before them. The tremulous answer was in the affirmative.

Without any circumlocution, the lady then, in prompt and decided terms, told the fellow the cause of her errand. He waited to hear her through, answered not a word, sat the light down on a table in the hall, ran upstairs, and in a moment more returned with the watch, which he gave into the lady's hands. The lady then immediately left the place, the youth accompanying her.

The next morning she had another conversation with the young novice in wickedness. She spoke to him as a sorrowing mother would speak to a beloved son. He expressed contrition, and made vows of amendment. He left the house, promising to return again at dinner. From that time to this, she has not seen him, or heard from him more.

We have given this long story, every syllable of which is true, partly as an exposure of what vicious tricks there are going on among us, and partly as a caution to parents in this country. Hundreds of young fellows are lost by the carelessness of people in letting their sons be placed where temptation surrounds every side, as in the case of the youth whose history has been given.

Very likely, the villainous swindlers have him in their clutches again, and will effectually prevent a second relapse into virtue. The lady in question learnt not sufficient of his history to be able to tell where his parents or relations reside; consequently, she cannot, as she anxiously desires to do, give them information upon the subject by letter.

[MARCH 24, 1842]

FLOWERS

In walking along the streets of our city, we frequently have occasion to stop and admire beautiful plants and blooming flowers, exhibited in parlor windows. We never notice these lovely ornaments but we internally come to the conclusion that within the same house there resides some girl even more lovely; and we feel greatly inclined to "just step in," and see if there is any chance for a forlorn bachelor.

In all soberness, however, it is a pleasant and a cheerful thing, to see these delicate beauties, (the flowers, we mean,) in a city house. It infers that in that house, there exist some feelings apart from the gross ones that sully most human minds; and that refinement and taste for natural simplicity are there.

Ladies of New York, be sure that hereafter you cultivate small shrubbery and plants.

NOTE.—Under privacy, reader, we expect Thorburn[12] and Niblo[13] to advertise in the Aurora after this.

[MARCH 24, 1842]

YESTERDAY

Another charming, delicious, summer like day have we had. The air was bland and clear, the sun shone out, and every body came forth to enjoy the beauty of the season.

It is a pleasant thing to see crowds of well dressed men and women, with smiling faces, promenading our streets or our public grounds. And the little children! the fat, fresh, clean, healthy, merry

little children—it is better than splendor to look at them and their
gambols. What heart so gross, what brain so deficient in loveable-
ness, as not to be pleased with the spectacle of little children at play?

Before long it will be time for the trees and grass on the Battery,
Park, and so forth, to put forth their foliage. And then the poor
man and his little flock may enjoy a cheap treat (none the less
precious because it is cheap) in passing a couple of hours there on
Sunday.

We should be better pleased were our city government to have
more parks—more open places, where a man may look a few rods
about him, and his gaze not be intercepted by brick walls, and
chimneys, and fences.

[MARCH 28, 1842]

A PEEP AT THE ISRAELITES

For the first time in our life, we went, on Saturday morning last,
to spend an hour in a Jewish synagogue. Accompanied by a friend,
and starting at 10 o'clock, we wended our way through Centre
street, from thence into Crosby,[14] in which, a block or two above
Grand, we found the place of our destination. The front to the street
was boarded by a high fence, with banister work on top. Passing
through a gate, and down two or three rods by the side of the building, we went up the steps of a porch in the rear, where we found the
entrance.

Fearful lest we should go somewhere or do something that might
be totally malapropos, we waited a few moments, until, seeing a
gentleman enter, we followed him through a side door into the main
body of the house. There, we were politely ushered to a convenient
seat, from whence we had a fair view of all the performances.

The whole scene was entirely new; never had we beheld any thing
of a similar description before. The congregation (we don't know
what other word to use) were all standing, each one with his hat
on. A white silken mantle, somewhat like a scarf, was worn by every
person; it encircled the neck, falling down the back, and the ends
in front reaching to the floor. In the middle of the room was a raised
platform about four yards square, with heavy balustrade of bronze
work and mahogany around it. Upon the centre of this platform
was a figure which, by the voice coming from it, we knew to be a
man. None of the lineaments of the human form, however, were
visible; for one of the large silk mantles alluded to was thrown
over his head, and completely shrouded him. He was speaking; but

as his language was Hebrew, we could not understand a word he uttered.

At the further end of the room stood an erection very much resembling the front that pictures give the ancient Parthenon. Under it was a semi circular partitioned enclosure, of panelled wood, which from the ornaments and expensive tracery lavished upon the whole affair, seemed intended to contain something either very valuable, or very sacred. Upon the platform which made part of this structure, there was another figure standing, half shrouded in a white mantle, like the personage before described. He was also speaking.

And there we were amid the Jews worshipping in their temple. The people of Solomon and Saul, of Ruth and Mary Magdalene, of the traitor Judas, and John, the beloved Son of God—the people of the very Christ himself—these were they who stood around. And they were speaking in the same tones as those which at night bade the shepherds to follow the guidance of the star in the east—the same tones which Jonathan and Saul used in their beautiful friendship—which sounded out from the plaintive Hagar in the wilderness —through which Absalom, "that too beauteous boy," made rebellion against his father—with which the widow's son, who was dead, and brought to life again, gladdened his desolate mother's heart;— the tones and the native language of the holy Psalmist, the lovely Rebecca of Scott, and the malignant Shylock of Shakespeare.

And here was a remnant of the mighty nation, who routed the warlike dwellers in Canaan, and who received the Law from the great I Am upon the mountain of clouds;—their ancient pride swept to the winds—their name a jeering and mark for contempt—their might humbled, their old homes taken by the hand of the spoiler, and dark frowns for ages spread around them;—yet here, scoffed, scouted, and scorned, they came, to worship their God after the manner of their ancestors.

The heart within us felt awed as in the presence of memorials from an age that had passed away centuries ago. The strange and discordant tongue—the mystery, and all the associations that crowded themselves in troops upon our mind—made a thrilling sensation to creep through every nerve. It was indeed a sight well calculated to impress the mind with an unwonted tone.

As our account has already stretched to the limits beyond which it is not judicious to go in a paper like ours, we shall give the remainder of what we saw during our stay at the synagogue, in the *Aurora* tomorrow.

[MARCH 28, 1842]

DOINGS AT THE SYNAGOGUE

We continue our account of what we saw on Saturday, during our visit to the Jews' synagogue in Crosby street. It may perhaps be well to say here, that we had no one to explain to us what we saw, and as the whole scene from beginning to end resembled nothing that we had ever seen before, our relation professes to give merely the scene as it appears to the eyes of an utter stranger. Very likely we may make some awkward blunders; but nevertheless the reader shall have our "first impressions."

After the performance had continued for some time as we described it in yesterday's Aurora, some of the Jews went up to the semicircular panel work before mentioned, unlocked it, and opened the doors. Three or four of them took from the inclosure certain contrivances, which we dare hardly pretend to describe, for fear of bungling in the attempt. As near as we can now recollect, they resembled in shape large sugar loaves; and each had an ornamental and fantastic affair made of silver and glass upon its top.[15] These were brought up to the platform in the centre, and each of the silver ornaments we have described was taken from the top of the sugar loaf structure, and put upon the desk in front.

The priest then raised aloft a large scroll of parchment, probably the sacred law—wafting it around so that the people could see it in all parts of the house. All this while he uttered a kind of chant, to which the men and women made responses.

We saw M. M. Noah,[16] of the sessions court, among the Jews present. He officiated upon the platform in some of the ceremonies.

The main floor, on which we were, was occupied exclusively by men. There was a gallery over it filled with women—dark-eyed Jewesses, most of them dressed in black, and a few strangers, attracted there probably by curiosity.

The spectacle in the gallery was by no means the most unpleasing sight in the whole proceeding. Up aloft they seemed to pay as reverent heed to the exercises as in any part of the congregation. We found ourselves casting our glances thither quite frequently; perhaps this may account for our not having distinct recollection of the whole matter.

The personage who appeared to officiate as the high priest continued his chant, and the people their responses. Every now and then, while the parchment scroll was upon the desk, and unrolled before the priest, individuals from the congregation would step forward, and upon the platform, and speak to the priest. Then, while they stood by and looked on, he would read them something from

the parchment spread out upon the desk. For five minutes, perhaps,
this would last; and then another person would come up and go
through the same ceremony.

Of course, to our perceptions, the whole affair had much the aspect of an unintelligible mummery. Still we could not divest ourselves of the thought that we were amid the people of ancient Jewry;
the people who had kept themselves apart from the contagion of the
world, and adhered strictly to the customs, and observances, and
laws of their forefathers.

Once or twice we allowed fancy to have its unchecked flow. The
then and there scene vanished from our eyes; the uncouth jabber,
and the fantastic garb of the worshippers were heard and seen no
more. We were in the holy city. The palaces of the haughty nobles
—the magnificent temple which the Jews loved as the apple of their
eye—the streets and the houses, and the public places—all, all, were
there. And along the public thoroughfare came trailingly a solemn
group. In the centre was a pale being with a crown of thorns bound
round his forehead, and blood trickling down his brow. It was the
Holy Savior of Man, bearing the cross upon his shoulder. And as
he passed, the mob scouted and reviled him—his very friends
thought it scorn to recognize him; all but *one*, a woman, who followed him even to the place of his crucifixion.

We did not wait to see the conclusion of the exercises. After a
stay of more than an hour, feeling somewhat wearied by the continuance of vocal utterance, which we could not take the meaning
of, we left the place.

[MARCH 29, 1842]

A PEEP IN AT HUDSON'S ROOMS

By way of relieving a sentimental stroll yesterday afternoon, we
dropped in at Hudson & Ottingnon's gymnasium, on the corner of
Chambers street and Broadway.

After a few shots in the pistol gallery, we walked into the large
hall to observe the feats of those who were practicing on the various
gymnastic apparatus it contains. One pupil was swinging himself
across the room with his hands on the rungs of an elevated ladder;
another was laboring up a smooth pole with all the eagerness of a
man struggling for life; a third was performing a similar effort on
a loose dangling rope, while some five or six couples were darting
huge buckskin gloves into each other with the most untiring per-

severance. After an hour's lounge, during which we effectually banished our threatened melancholy, we bid the gentlemanly proprietors good bye, resolved to recommend the use of their excellent establishment to all dyspeptic and misanthropic young gentlemen, as well as all those who have a desire to secure artistical instruction in the science of self defense.

[MARCH 29, 1842]

CENTRE MARKET FESTIVAL

We strolled in for ten minutes last evening to the festival at Centre market. It was quite a magnificent affair. Large numbers of ladies, young, middle aged, and even old, were there. We noticed some whose beauty would bear comparison with the greatest belles of New York. They lined the sides of the tables, which were spread with choice eatables, and added greatly (the ladies, we mean, not the eatables) to the interest and amusement of the occasion.

The band played several airs, after which there was an address, then an ode, and then another address, during which we left.

Banners and pictures ornamented the principal room, and everything seemed to go off with the utmost cheerfulness and eclat. We would suggest to the Washingtonians,[17] however, that they teach politeness to their doorkeepers. We had to chaffer ten minutes before admittance. When any one connected with the Aurora takes the trouble to visit public places—he considers that if there is any favor in the matter, it certainly does not come from them to him.[18]

[MARCH 30, 1842]

TEMPERANCE AMONG THE FIREMEN!

Yesterday was a great time with the New York temperance societies, as will be seen by a report on our first page, furnished us by the editor of the Washingtonian.[19] They had processions, and meetings, and orations, and festivals, and banners displayed, and music, and a grand blow out at night to cap the whole. We stood upon the steps of the City Hall about 4 o'clock in the afternoon, and saw the passage of the grand procession, which certainly cut a very respectable figure. Thousands of people were gathered together in the Park to witness the scene.

First came a banner bearing the head of Washington, immediately after which were a body of firemen. Whether it be a whim, or from some more tangible cause, we do have a fondness for the New York firemen. They are mostly fine, stalwart, handsome young men; and in their close fitting dresses and red shirts, we never behold them, but the Roman gladiators and the Olympian games are brought to our mind. We question whether any city in the world can turn out a more manly set of young fellows. It is honorable to them, that they engage in this temperance movement. With the generosity and ardent devotedness of youth, they throw themselves, heart and soul, into the cause. This is a great thing gained. Once make temperance a favorite and fashionable custom among the young men of our city, and the whole conquest is over,—the enemy is vanquished.

After the firemen came an immense number of citizens, formerly intemperate men, but now worthy members of society. There was a beautiful flag representing a female figure, and on each side a gushing spring of water. Then the junior temperance societies, with a banner inscribed, "beware of the first glass!" A number of sailors followed. Then more firemen, with a beautiful hose cart, No. 18, we believe. The hatters' association made a very respectable appearance, as also did the Newark society and the Chelsea society. The banners had a great many quaint devices. One we noticed bearing a sheaf of grain, and the motto, "If you eat me, I am life; if you drink me, I am death."

[MARCH 30, 1842]

SCENES OF LAST NIGHT[20]

Between seven and eight o'clock last evening we visited the scene of the fire in Broome and Delancy streets. For several blocks before arriving there, our passage was impeded by squads of people hurrying to and fro with rapid and eager pace. Women carrying small bundles—men with heated and sweaty faces—little children, many of them weeping and sobbing—met us every rod or two. Then there were stacks of furniture upon the sidewalks and even in the street; puddles of water, and frequent lengths of hose-pipe endangered the pedestrian's safety; and the hubbub, the trumpets of the engine foremen, the crackling of the flames, and the lamentations of those who were made homeless by the conflagration—all sounded louder and louder as we approached, and at last grew to one continued and deafening din.

It was a horrible yet magnificent sight! When our eyes caught a full view of it, we beheld a space of several acres, all covered with smouldering ruins, mortar, red hot embers, piles of smoking half burnt walls—a sight to make a man's heart sick, and keep him awake at night, when lying in his bed.

We stood on the south side of Broome street. In every direction around, except the opposite front, there was one compact mass of human flesh—upon the stoops, and along the side walks, and blocking up the street, even to the edge of where the flames were raging. The houses at our right were as yet unharmed, with the exception of blistered paint and window glass cracked by the strong heat over the way. We looked through those windows into the rooms within. The walls were bare and naked; no furniture, no inhabitant, no signs of occupancy or life, but every thing bearing the stamp of desolation and flight!

Every now and then would come a suffocating whirlwind of smoke and burning sparks. Yet we stood our ground—we and the mass— silent, and gazing with awful admiration upon the wreck and the brightness before us. The red flames rolled up the sides of the houses, newly caught, like the forked tongues of serpents licking their prey. It was terribly grand! And then all the noise would cease, and for many minutes nothing would break in upon silence, except the hoarse voices of the engines and their subordinates, and the hissing of the fire. A few moments more, and the clatter and clang sounded out again with redoubled loudness.

The most pitiful thing in the whole affair, was the sight of shivering women, their eyes red with tears, and many of them dashing wildly through the crowd, in search, no doubt, of some member of their family, who, for what they knew, might be buried neath the smoking ruins near by. Of all the sorrowful spectacles in God's world, perhaps no one is more sorrowful than such as this!

And those crumbled ashes! What comforts were entombed there —what memories of affection and companionship, and brotherhood —what preparation never to be consummated—what hopes never to see their own fruition—fell down as the walls and the floors fell down, and were crushed as they were crushed! But twelve hours before, the sun rose pleasantly—all promised fair, and no danger clouded the clearness of hope's horizon. The most distant idea of all this misery, it entered into the brain of no man to conceive. *Now*, what a change! People who commenced the day moderately rich, closed it penniless. Those that had a house to shelter them at sunrise, at sunset owned no pillow whereon to lay their heads. Wives and husbands who parted in the morning with jocund words, met at night to mingle their groans together, and to grieve over blighted prospects.

On the minds of hundreds there, no doubt, these and similar reflections forced themselves. We saw it in the sombre countenances of the spectators—their fixed look; and heard it in their conversation one to another. And so, elbowing and pushing our way for many rods through the crowd, we at last made out to get once more where the air was less hot and stifling, and the press of the people less intense.

On our way down, we stopped in for a while at the Temperance Hall in Grand street, where there appeared to be a large meeting. The apartment was filled with an assemblage of both sexes. A speaker, whose name we understood as Capt. Wisdom, was speaking from the platform. His language seemed totally deficient in polish and in grammatical correctness; but he evidently *felt* what he was saying, and desired to do as much good as possible. No doubt, the method of Mr. Wisdom is far more effective for the sphere it moves in, than a more refined style. An address by a person whose tongue had a broad foreign accent, followed Mr. W. This man gave his "experience," and descanted in enthusiastic terms on the great blessing the temperance cause had been to him. He was a very uncouth speaker. Yet, how all the boundaries of taste, all the laws of conventional usage, are leaped over, in oratory, by deep feeling and ardent sincerity. Every hearer in the room, assuredly, was thrilled to the heart by portions of this uneducated man's remarks. For our part, we were never more interested in our life.

Then there was music. A choir, composed mainly of ladies, sang an ode—and a company of fine looking firemen variefied the exercises with a temperance glee.

As we left the house, we could not help wondering at the mighty enthusiasm which all there, men, women and children, seemed to be imbued with. Success to the cause! May the blessings that have followed in its path, thus far, be but the harbinger—a shadow of the hundred fold glory that is coming!

[APRIL 1, 1842]

[GUARDIANS AT THE GRAVE[21]]

*"On stepping into the ground at the corner of Chrystie and De-
lancy streets, we found a woman armed with a pistol, guarding the
grave of her husband and children."*

The above paragraph we cut from a report of the proceedings at
Chrystie street grave yard day before yesterday. It may possibly not
be known to all our readers that in the eastern section of the city
great excitement has been raging among the people, because a
chartered company have taken steps to break up the ground of a
large grave yard there, for purposes of building upon the locality it
occupies. Among the numbers who "turned out" on the occasion,
appears to have been the woman mentioned in the lines which head
this article.

A mysterious thing is woman's love! Here comes a widow, her
husband dead, perhaps, for years and years—and at the most distant
rumor of insult offered to his shapeless and decayed ashes, the old
tenderness and the old sympathies are roused again! Pale with excitement, she arms herself with deadly weapons, and stands over
his grave, and the graves of her children, angry, like a tigress at
bay. Law, the customs of men, the limit that conventional forms
have marked—all are disregarded. No thought enters her mind,
but the engrossing fear that her dear ones are threatened with insult,
and that it is her duty to protect them.

And who, viewing this, can say that there are not glorious and
beautiful dispositions in the human heart? No prospect of making
money—no gross ideas of winning or losing lucre—called this
gathering together. Their bond of union was made sacred through
the memory of past love—the love of friends and relatives, dead and
laid away to their long sleep.

We can sympathise with these people. We were thrilled at reading the anecdote given above. For there is in every man's breast a
sentiment which leads him to regard with horror any desecration of
the dark and ghostly grave. Even the savages are not devoid of this
feeling.

Coarse indeed must be the character, and callous the soul, that
would touch sorely upon these hallowed sympathies.

[APRIL 1, 1842]

THE PARK MEETING

At the appointed hour, 5 o'clock yesterday afternoon, a collection of people began to congregate in the Park, for the purpose of taking measures to prevent the desecration of the graves in the church yard of Chrystie and Delancy streets. Alderman Purdy was appointed to preside over the meeting.

Mr. Job Haskell rose to address the assemblage. He said that not a long time had passed away since his own wife was buried in the contested ground. She was there now. And he appealed to any man if, under the circumstances, he was not justified in using warm language to mark his sense of his wickedness of the conduct of those who would infringe on the repose of those tombs. Mr. Haskell said that day before yesterday afternoon he came down to the Park for the purpose of attending the meeting appointed to take place there—that while thus away from his home, the fire broke out which devasted a large portion of that neighborhood, his house among others being burnt to the ground. Mr. H. hoped that the meeting would take strong steps for the furtherance of the objects which they so anxiously desired to see attained.

Mr. Taylor, editor of the Commercial Transcript, next made a few remarks. He stated that he had no personal interest in the controversy; but he felt in his breast that the last resting spot of man should not be disturbed. He related a thrilling account, which we alluded to in our paper of yesterday, of the woman who, on Wednesday, was seen guarding the grave of her relatives with a loaded pistol. Mr. Taylor said that the same pistol was used by the woman's husband in the last war—used to defend the land from foreign invasion. Mr. T. spoke very warmly and ardently.

A great portion of the audience were women. We noticed tears in the eyes of many—no doubt called up by the associations of thought that they could not help.

We did not stay to see the conclusion of the meeting. It was evident that there was a strong and enthusiastic determination to defend the graves from violation, at all hazards. It was proposed to appoint a committee for the purpose of proceeding to Albany and asking the passage of a law that would meet the requirements of the case.

[APRIL 2, 1842]

[A DISGRACEFUL PROCEEDING] [22]

We proceed this morning to make some remarks upon the disgraceful proceedings in relation to the Baptist grave yard in Chrystie street—that have caused so much excitement of late in the eastern section of the city.

If we were asked the particular trait of national character from which might be apprehended the greatest evil to the land, we should unhesitatingly point to the strife for gain which of late years has marked, and now marks, the American people. This unholy spirit seems to have no bound or check. It leads yearly to the commission, among us, of the most abominable actions. It has built up those paper money bubbles, which daily practice, in the face of day, frauds and violations of their engagements, that ought to make the cheek of every upright man blush with indignation. It forms insolent and selfish cliques, that stand out against the government itself, and laugh at punishment. It imbues the popular mind with a disposition to connive at villany, if joined with wealth—to palliate crime, if its consequences are estate—to smile gently at a swindler, if he has only been a swindler of millions.

Even the battle spots where our old soldiers fought and died, are not beyond the reach of this pollution. The very hill made sacred by the blood of freedom's earliest martyrs, is sold and trafficked for.

But it has been reserved for *our city* to put the damning climax to these deeds that disgrace humanity. A set of miserable wretches —through courtesy, we suppose, passing in the world as *gentlemen* —have, within the past fortnight, rendered themselves infamous by desecrating the very *grave*, in order to add something to their ill won heaps of gold. We are almost at a loss for terms of opprobrium severe enough to characterise the conduct of these mean and brutal money worshippers. Do they pretend to possess the souls of men? After thus becoming a scandal and a disgrace to nature—after thus doing what the very wickedest criminal at Sing Sing would scorn— they might as well go and buy ropes and hang themselves; for they surely cannot expect hereafter that which decent men deserve, as honor, love, obedience, troops of friends.

These creatures actually set people to work with spades and pick-axes to dig down and pitch out the decayed relics of bodies buried there Fleshless bones, and ghastly skeltons, and skulls with the hair still attached to them, and the brittle relics of young infants, and the shrouded ashes of age, and forms of once beautiful maidens, now putrid in corruption—all these, fearful and sickening, and making the very heart of the looker on to thrill with horror—were struck in by the cold steel, and pitched to and fro, as loafers pitch pennies upon the dock.

Let the finger of scorn and indignation be pointed at these men. Let popular opinion show them what reward is meted out to soulless brutes, who outrage every pure and gentle feeling of the soul—every sentiment of love, every remnant of the perfection that was Adam's in Eden!

[APRIL 5, 1842]

"MARBLE TIME" IN THE PARK

Reader, let us take a lounge together. Be'st thou gentle lady, or busy merchant, or indolent idler, or working man, or student—it will do thee no harm. Nor, if a high bred dame, needest thou start at our familiarity; we only ask thee to lock arms with us—in imagination. And as the time of an editor is precious, and we cannot circulate very far, we will descend from our sanctum, exit, cross over to the iron gate opposite, and enter the Park.

Evidences of the coming summer are around us. The grass has just put on a delicate green, buds are upon the tips of the branches, and the sun beats down with an ardent warmth upon us. The air is balmy and delicious. Is it not pleasant to be, once in a while, where your prospect is unintercepted by walls and stacks of chimneys within a dozen arms' length?

It is "marble time"; and in many a nook and sunny spot around, we observe groups of the little people playing at that time honored divertisement. Let us stop a while, and observe yon busy squad to the left. What a heterogeneous mixture And what fine, healthy, dirty, bright eyed, mischievous little devils most of them are! We are among them; silence and attention!

A large ring of two yards in diameter encircles a smaller ring in the center, which latter encircles ten or fifteen marbles. "I'm first!" exclaims an urchin, whose shirt tail is sticking out from a tear in his trousers—"I'm first," and down he bends, at the outer ring, with his marble between his thumb nail and the end of the second finger. For a moment he waits, taking aim, as it were—leans his head slightly one side, cocks his eye with a knowing half wink, and surveys the whole bearing of the ground. Then with a firm, nervous, quick jerk of the outer joint of the thumb, he sends the pebble forward. Aha! it scatters the heap "put in" by the other boys, and one of the marbles

has rolled completely out of the large ring. He pockets it, and by the
laws of the game, has a right to a second trial. Again he bends; but
now, elated with success, neglects his former cautiousness. Long
practice, however, has made his aim expert and mere habit; he scatters the heap, as before—but none of them goes beyond the ring.

Next comes a red haired young gentleman, whose hat, being marvellous scant of brim, and, moreover, intended originally for a
caput twice the size of its present wearer's, slides down every now
and then over his eyes, and rests upon the bridge of his nose—much
to the red haired young gentleman's annoyance and tribulation. Ere
he kneels him upon the ring, he gives his head a quick toss, by which
he gains temporary relief from the grief above alluded to.

"Knuckle down to taw!" ejaculates one of the players.

Now, lest the unitiated should not comprehend the meaning conveyed by the foregoing phrase, it may be well to say that "knuckle
down to taw!" is equivalent to "plant your hand on the ring, fairly!"
words which imply that the individual to whom they are spoken, is
disposed to take some undue unfair advantage. We would by no
means assert that the red haired young gentleman *was* disposed to
take such advantage; that is a point which we think proper to leave
to the sagacity of the reader. And here, were we disposed to be phil-
osophical, we might expatiate at full length on the propriety of knowing for sure, before you give decision upon a mooted point. We for-
bear.

The marble of the red haired young gentleman flies wide of its
mark. It takes no effect at all.

And then come brown haired young gentlemen, and dark haired
young gentlemen, and young gentlemen with snub noses, and young
gentlemen with sharp noses, and, in short, young gentlemen of all
qualities and ages, from the thick lipped negro sweep to the aristocratic truant from the college high school a few rods to the north.

What troops of children, large and small, appear on every side!
Were it amiss to look on them, engaged as they are so earnestly—
as but mimics of the strife that occupies our advanced years! And
the "knuckle down to taw!" and the "fen scrapins "—have they not
their counterpart in manhood?

How ardent the little gamesters are! How pleased at gaining a
spherical moiety of clay—and how cast down at losing it! Thus it
is. In our greener age, we pursue shadows and toys; in maturity, the
toil and the sweat and the fever are for benefits as intangible, and
phantom gewgaws, intrinsically as valueless as the objects of our
youth. Why should we smile at the zeal and irritability of children?
We daily chase gilded butterflies. In our common walks—in the path

of ordinary business, we spend precious time, and godlike capacities, and advantages of fortune, to reach some goal where, when we arrive, we turn sick with disappointment and disgust at its not conferring the blessings we most foolishly expected.

[APRIL 4, 1842]

[A LAZY DAY]

Reader, we fear you have, by way of novelty, a *poor Aurora* this morning. We felt dull and inactive all yesterday, "pottered" as Fanny Kemble[23] would express it, during the earlier hours of the day; and after dinner, (we dine at 2) and chatting fifteen minutes, (for the benefit of digestion) we came round to our accustomed editorial nook, and took up the pen, intending to dash into Bishop Hughes,[24] Webster,[25] or Justice Matsell,[26] and knock those worthies into a disarranged chapeau. But it was no go! We had the pleasant influences of a good dinner moving our breast to love everything! and be indulgent toward every body, (O! Mrs. C.[27] you little know what power you and the cook down below have upon the popular pulse, as said pulse is acted on through Aurora!) and so we repented us, and politely desisted from our pugnacious intentions.

Then finding it impossible to do anything either in the way of "heavy business," or humor, we took our cane, (a heavy, dark beautifully polished, hook ended one,) and our hat, (a plain, neat fashionable one, from Banta's, 130 Chatham street, which we got gratis, on the strength of giving him this puff,) and sauntered forth to have a stroll down Broadway to the Battery.[28] Strangely enough, nobody stared at us with admiration—nobody said "there goes *the* Whitman, of Aurora!"—nobody ran after us to take a better, and second better look—no ladies turned their beautiful necks and smiled at us—no apple women became pale with awe—no news boys stopped, and trembled, and took off their hats, and cried "behold the man what uses up the Great Bamboozle!"[29]—no person wheeled out of our path deferentially—but on we went, swinging our stick, (the before mentioned dark and polished one,) in our right hand—and with our left hand tastily thrust in its appropriate pocket, in our frock coat, (a gray one.)

Well, (are you interested, dear reader?) in due time we arrived at the ponderous iron gates which give ingress to the Battery. We entered. We strolled along—casting a side glance now and then at the beautiful green that was just "being put on" by the grass—and arrived, after a while, at the south extreme of Gotham's glorious promenade. Then we turned. We walked slowly and lazily back, enjoying the fresh air, and the delicious sunshine, and the intoxicating sweetness of the beauty of nature that appeared all around.

A number of children were at play—some kind of a game which required that they should take each others' hand and spread themselves so as to make a large ring. When we came up, they were just in the crisis of their game, and occupying clear across the walk.

"Ah!" said one, with a peevish air, to a companion, "we shall have to break the line. There comes a gentleman."

The boy spoken to was a fine, handsome fellow, of twelve or thirteen years. He turned and looked at us for a moment; then the expression changed, and his face greeted ours with an arch confiding smile, as much as to say "I know, my dear sir, you are too good natured to disturb us, merely to save the trouble of turning out a step." It is needless to add, we *did* turn out. What wonderful powers children have of discriminating who is possessed of a courteous, kindly, manful and creditable disposition!

Then we came up, and out, and along Broadway, to whence we started. And for the next two or three hours, we possess no recollection of having done anything in particular. And at half past 8, P. M. (fifteen minutes before this present writing) the chilling consciousness came over us that we hadn't written anything for a leader. And so we concocted the foregoing (what were you about, at half past 8, last night, dear reader?)

And all we have to add is, that if you read it over a second time you will find more meaning in it, than you might at first imagine.

[APRIL 6, 1842]

SOMETHING WORTH PERUSAL

We took our usual stroll down Broadway a little while after noon, yesterday. Gods! what a glorious morning it was! Just enough of enervating, voluptuous heat—and just enough breeze to fill the wings of the zephyrs—and just enough sunshine to reflect a sparkle in the eyes of beautiful women—and just enough people walking on the pave to make one continued, ceaseless, devilish provoking, delicious, glorious jam!

Wasn't it brave! And *didn't* we laugh (not outwardly—that would

have been vulgar; but in the inward soul's bedchamber) with very
excess of delight and gladness? O, it is a beautiful world we live in,
after all! The All Bounteous has made for us pleasures that are pure
—joys which pall not, and are fresh ever—balmy air, and the fantastic drapery of clouds, and the sight of mighty waters, and a thousand influences, solemn and sweet, that forbid their entertainment
to no man, but are spread by God, as a banquet where all may come,
and none shall be thrust aside.

Just off against Grace Church, we met a pale, tall, delicate girl,
dressed fashionably, yet very neatly. She had her veil only half drawn
over her face; and as we looked, we beheld one of the most lovely,
intellectually feminine countenances our sight was ever blessed with.
We never professed to be very susceptible to the tender passion—but
really those starlike eyes! and that queenly neck! and those luscious
lips! O, we'd better stop—for if we go on, we shall . . .

Then, down upon the Battery. We found the grass more darkly
colored than the day before; and as we looked up to the trees overhead, we noticed swelling buds and leaves just breaking out. And so,
on we went, with one hand in the side pocket of our coat, (*the* grey
one,) and shortly arrived at the heavy balustrade which runs along
on the edge of the flagstones. We stopped, and leaned upon the stout
wooden rail, and directed our gaze, half indolently, half sentiment-
ally, far out over the waters of the dark green bay that stretched before us. It was a cheerful sight, that river. They tell us that our land
is in difficulty—that the republic is bankrupt and starving. Let us
laugh them to scorn! Behold those ponderous masts—that sloop
from Albany with flours and meats—that mighty fleet of fat looking
craft, some with lowing kine, sheep and other butcher ware—some
with fish, the savory shad, and the delicious oyster—and the hale,
thick limbed, amphibious creatures, man and boy, that are on board
them.

Despair, indeed! Send sombre thoughts to the devil—we'll none
of them, saith the heart within us. Have we not youth, and health,
and no memory of guilty crimes committed, and a fair field, and the
whole field before us? Again, we say, send care to the devil!

When our inclinations informed us that we felt disposed to slope,
we turned, and sauntered listlessly up, and out the iron gates, and
along Broadway. For a while nothing particular attracted our attention. We had arrived at that section of our walk whereabout it became necessary for us to pass the Courtlandt street crossing, when
we saw——

Who can describe it? Yes *it!* for though the creature had shape,
if shape it might be called which shape had none, except that given

to it by the tailor, by padding, by corsets, by ligaments, and by straps—or substance might be called that brainless was—yet surely the thing——

Courtlandt street corner certainly was the place; we can't be mistaken about *that*. And the ——, the *stranger* undoubtedly did make his appearance *there*. His lower half, truly, was unexceptionable, and his coat faultless; but his—his——

Reader, look at him!

There, you have it—the cat's out of the bag![30] As the writer of laconics say, farther comment is unnecessary. We will just add, however, that we did not faint, *nor* stagger, *nor* howl. We did *not* cast one longing, look behind—but we half twisted our neck, to cast *two*, right and left.

Talk of gentlemen fleeing from a mad dog—of locomotives—of race horses, indeed! How *we* streaked it!

[APRIL 7, 1842]

PLAYING IN THE PARK

It is customary for numbers of boys, of pleasant days, to congregate in the Park, and amuse themselves by running races, trundling hoops, playing marbles, and the like. Most of these are poor ragged little devils, with plenty of dirt, and plenty of the signs of poverty about them. They offend nobody, interfere with nobody, and generate no evil to themselves in these innocent and wholesome amusements. Yet it is customary for one or two understrappers who have charge of the Park, to rush into the midst of the squads of youngsters, beat them with rattans, and cuff them, and disperse them. It may be thought a small matter to speak about, but we nevertheless shall take the liberty of saying that it is a useless and brutal proceeding. Because these children are poor, dirty, and ragged, that is no reason why they should be whipped in this manner, and prevented from pursuing their little amusements. On the Battery, and in other public grounds, any quantity of the offspring of the rich and fashionable may be daily seen playing and no objection made. Such conduct may hardly have the effect of teaching the proper moral to young *republicans*.

[APRIL 12, 1842]

SENTIMENT AND A SAUNTER

With the passage of the sun over its meridian, yesterday, we sauntered out of the Aurora office, through the Park, and across the flagstones that lead from the two western gates to the opposite side of
Broadway. A brown faced personage, dressed in blue, with a cloth
cap and a gold band around it, was standing on the steps of the lordly Astor. He appeared quite solitary and alone; his hands were fold-
ed in a melancholy manner under the tail of his coat, and he gazed
abstractedly upon the busy current that coursed beneath him. By the
erectness of his mien, and particularly by the brass buttons upon his
garments, we felt pretty safe in setting him down as the American
navy.

On we went. As we passed Colman's, we stopped a moment to look
at the prints of "Abelard and Heloise," and at some scripture pieces,
that ornamented the bow windows. What soft and sunny coloring,
and how smoothly the shades of light and darkness fell upon the proper points of the picture! And those hapless lovers—whose heart
might not melt in sympathising sorrow at the story of their affection
—affection bestowed "not wisely, but too well?" Powerful is the
pen! There in Italy, some hundred years ago, lived an obscure
young man, who loved as obscure a maiden. Thousands of cases, just
like theirs, have occurred, and are occurring; yet preserved by the
cunning magic of the author's quill, the history of Abelard and
Heloise will continue among us, and through after ages, as now, will
touch chords in the soul, and create pity for their miseries. Surely
no weapon so mighty as the *pen*, wielded by a master hand!

Again we wended on. The weather was delicious; beautiful sunshine overhead—balmy, fragrant air—and the sight of many happy
faces—all contributed to make the spectacle one of cheerfulness and
grace. Near the City Hotel we passed a man with the face of a goat;
his upper lip was completely covered with black bushy hair, as were
also his jaws and under his chin. People turned round in their walk
to look at the creature. It is an abominable practice, this, of convert-
ing a human countenance into a locomotive map! Wasn't it Paulding, when he was navy secretary, who issued the order for general
shearing and cropping of these diabolical appendages? It would be
matter for erudite investigation to discover what concert there is between this movement and the decline of barrelled hair.

The Globe Hotel is a tasty structure, as far as we can judge from
an outside view. Those neat lamps, and the quietly fashionable air of
the whole place, suits our ideas to an iota. There is a kind of rich
unostentation in the appearance of the Globe, which it might not be

amiss for "some people" to imitate. We mean this latter hint for pre-
tensive parvenues—not hotel keepers.

Many of both sexes, fashionable ladies, well dressed men, a
sprinkling of loafers, and rather more than the usual quantity of
"people from the country," (you can always tell a rustic in Broadway, from his ill-at-easeness)—were out upon the pave. We cast list-
less glances, at the mingled mass. At everything that was to be seen
around—and so sauntered down to Castle Garden entrance.

Then we turned and came slowly back to the place where we started, having spent an hour as pleasantly as a man could wish.

[APRIL 13, 1842]

THE HOUSE OF REFUGE

In the course of our peregrinations about town yesterday, to see
the humors of election, and the improvement in the uptown wards,
we dropped in at the very admirable establishment adjoining the
almshouse, which is known as the House of Refuge, but which is
solely under the control of the Society for the Reformation of Juven-
ile Delinquents.

We saw about two hundred lads, some of whom had been incipient
thieves, and all, perhaps, more or less steeped in that vice, which
runs through the Atlantic cities—loaferism—reduced to a state of the
most perfect discipline. At a signal from the superintendent, Mr.
Terry, they were all mustered in less than two minutes, and formed
on parade, "en militaire," and after going through some portion of
the drill exercise, they marched into their dining hall with the most
admirable precision. Inside these *salle et manger* they took their
places, standing at the table, until all were mustered, and then, at a
signal from the chief officer of the establishment, grace was said, and
the boys all sat down to a plain but plentiful meal. Many of these
boys we recognized by their countenances as having been paraded in
the Sessions and before the Police, and were pleased to see a marked
improvement. For the meagre hand dog look of the loafer, they have
exchanged that of the student, and instead of the physiognomy of the
incipient abstractionist, we beheld the orderly demeanor of the rising mechanic. The male portion of the establishment—which is the
only portion we were permitted to see—appears to be admirable in
its discipline and arrangements, and we would say highly satisfactory
in its results. Such of our citizens who take an interest in the welfare

of the rising generation—and who is there that is not constantly
shocked by the sight of the youthful banditti which infest our high-
ways and byways?—should pay a visit to the House of Refuge.
[APRIL 13, 1842]

ABOUT CHILDREN

Coming out of the Aurora office between twelve and one o'clock
night before last, intending to wend our way homeward—on the
steps of a building between Tammany Hall and that which our printers occupy, we noticed a boy fast asleep. He might have been eleven
or twelve years old; and as we stooped over him we saw that he was
very ragged and very dirty. The glare of the gas lamp near by, light-
ing up the sleeper's face, showed features by no means deficient in
beauty and intelligence. We were about waking the youngster, when
a watchman who, unseen by us, had been leaning against the iron
lamp post, spoke and prevented the fulfillment of our intention. He
said that frequently, when the weather was not stormy or very cold,
the child would take an hour's sleep there; he was a newsboy—
patronised the Chatham theatre—his home was in the upper suburbs
of the city—and when kept late down town by his dramatic propen-
sities, he whiled away the intervening time until his morning work, in
the manner we then saw him. We inwardly breathed a benison upon
the slumbers and future lot of the poor devil, and walked forward.

We love children. Nor is it our custom to draw the line, and enter-
tain good feelings only for those that, being brought up in the lap of
fortune, are possessed of the polish of refinement, in their sphere.
Children—the poor man's or the rich man's—children, with all the
freshness, the alertness of nature—the dew, the bloom upon them, as
it were—how fond we have been of the mischief loving little creatures! They are fresh from the hands of Him whose architecture is
always perfect until desecrated by the conduct of the world. What
can be more merry than their voices, ringing out upon the air in
play—and what, than their innocent glee, better balm to the heart
of a man when he has been wearied with anger or disappointment?
The great novelist[31] of our day has shown a beautiful taste in select-
ing *children* for his heroes and heroines—if those two terms will apply. Previously, writers thought it was stooping too low; they considered the little people as too little for their pens. How true their
notions of the subject were, bear witness poor Oliver, and crazed
Barnaby, and pathetic Nell!

And the *death* of children—why do we never associate it with any thing terrible and ghastly—as we do with the death of grown people? Perhaps it is that in the latter case we know, however fair the past conduct of the deceased man or woman may have been, there was doubtless much guilt committed, either in disposition or in actual performance; for we sin every day of our lives. While in the other instance, the very extremest wrongs ever done by the dead child, were but airy follies, too trivial for account. One is the drying up of a clear transparent brooklet; and one the quenching of a river, more extensive, no doubt, but leaving upon its dry bed, the signs of hope wrecked, and trusted treasures betrayed. There are few prettier customs than that, said to be prevalent in some parts of Europe, of adorning the coffins of young people with flowers.[32]

A friend of ours, a parent of a large family, has among them one son[33] who is deaf and dumb from his birth. Having, from sympathy for this boy's hapless deprivation, shown him several kindnesses, such as win children's hearts—he always expresses the utmost pleasure at our visits to his father's house—and we are come to be on quite sociable terms together. Our little friend is very fond of paintings and engravings. He will spend whole hours in looking over a collection of them; and if he does not understand what they are meant to represent, he allows the company no peace until it is explained to him. During a call we made at his parents', a few days ago, he came running in with a picture he had just found in ransacking a portfolio, and which baffled him to comprehend. It was the crucifixion of Christ and the thieves. His head bound with thorns and leaning from the weight of his awful misery—large drops of blood mixing with the sweat that poured down upon his breast—the Man of Grief still bore upon his features the impress of a mighty and unconquerable, and benevolent mind. A thief was upon either side; one, in his agony, had drawn his limbs up as much as possible —and so faithful was the artist's skill, they seemed almost to be quivering in their torture.

We explained the scene as well as we could by signs to the boy. We showed how that wicked men had seized on the person of the holy Teacher, and had put him to death; how that, to make his misery more aggravated, they had crucified him between two most abandoned criminals. We pointed to the sun, and making a sweep with the arm from east to west, gave him to know that when the orb of day thrice crossed its circuit, the body of the murdered Nazarene burst the cerements of the grave, and, throwing aside the bonds of decay and death, rose to life and glory. It was very singular, and we could not help noticing it, that the mind of this dumb youth seemed to respond at once to the idea of a God. His looks were subdued and reverent; his appreciation of what we told him about the nature and mystery of the supreme power intuitive; his soul appeared awed within him; and as we went on to explain the affectionate disposition of the Great Master of the Apostles—how he gave assistance to the poor—how he comforted the sorrowful, and soothed the pains of sickness and guilt—how he called little children unto him—and how he met with no resting place whereon to lay his fainting limbs —-and was at last cruelly put to death, by agony the most excruciating—amid scoffs and revilings and ridicule—all this seemed to touch the child, even to his inmost heart.

[APRIL 16, 1842]

SNORING MADE MUSIC

Reader, was you ever so unfortunate as to be locked out, and put up at some lodging house where, much to your dismay, you are packed in a room containing some five or six single beds? Perhaps it is two o'clock in the morning—all the hotels are closed—and you have "Hobson's choice" in the matter, and it is this bed or none. You are tired, and long for rest. You get into the confines of sleep, when one of your fellow lodgers begins to snore; softly at first— a little higher—then a little stronger, till finally it resembles the grumbling of distant thunder. "Curse the fellow!" you mutter to yourself, and turn on the other side. Presently another joins in. His snoring is decidedly as disagreeable as the first, but his style is totally different—it sounds something like the short puffings of a steam engine.

"A damned comfortable sleep I am likely to have in this place!" you mutter again. But your troubles have only begun. A third joins in the chorus. His manner is essentially different from the others— a kind of long whine through the nose, ending with a snuffle. The music appears to be catching, for the whole five are now in rapid progress of *snorification*. You bolt upright in the bed, cursing your stars, night keys, and snorers. But it's no use—you are a martyr; you would be just as likely to sleep, if up to your middle in a marsh, surrounded by bull frogs. Gradually the sound becomes so extremely ludicrous to your ears, that you endeavor to draw the vocalists into tune.

SNORER NO. 1.—Bass; deep and strong voice, but rather ragged, thus—"Who-o-o caw, puff; who-o-o caw, puff."

SNORER NO. 2.—Tenor; voice decidedly melodious— "Huff whoo—huff whoo—huff whoo."

SNORER NO. 3.—Soprano; a canting, conventicle sound— "Whine whiff—whine whiff."

SNORER NO. 4.—Difficult to say what tones, but a mixture of all the above sounds. Now their dulcet notes join in sweet converse—

> Who-o-o caw, puff; who-o-o caw, puff;
> Huff whoo, huff whoo, huff whoo!
> Whine whiff, whine whiff!
> Puff, caw, huff, whine, whoo!
> &c. &c.

You can stand it no longer; you clap on your breeches and toggery just as day begins to dawn, and bolt from the premises more weary and tired than if you had walked the streets all night.

Mem.—Never sleep in a room with a strange lodger.

[APRIL 18, 1842]

THE SCHOOLS' HOLIDAY

Few days in the week are more interesting for a promenade in our stirring city than Saturday, for then the "schools are let loose," and pour their laughing congregations, into the great tide of mortality that flows through every avenue.

Last Saturday was a day of sunshine and soft air, and in our walk we met thousands and thousands of those joyous specimens of nature's fresh handiwork. Upon the Battery and in the various parks, hosts were assembled, exhibiting their agility in a hundred innocent and appropriate ways. The little girls would throw up their heads and shake their curling locks, and smile an apology for running against thoughtful old men and matrons, whose path they heedlessly trespassed on. Arch ones—well they knew that forgiveness was theirs!

Here a group were gazing upon the tempting array in the toy shops; there, others were feasting their eyes upon the display of variegated sweets in the confection windows.

Now, a little nymph, with her white pantalettes, and gypsy hat, and short frock, might be seen trundling her hoop, even among the dense human tide of Broadway, the thronging passers, as if by general consent, submitting to jostles from each other to prevent impeding her progress.

The good effect of this kindness toward the little folks will not be lost. It is teaching them, by the still but forcible language of example, one of the noblest lessons—how to be kind to others, to be amiable, obliging.

[APRIL 18, 1842]

BROADWAY YESTERDAY

We *did* think we had exhausted all the superlatives in praise of the aspect of Broadway of a pleasant afternoon. Yesterday, however, *was* too fine not to receive a passing notice.

We took a stroll down to the Battery, about four P. M. The crowd and the jam were tremendous. Hundreds of splendid women and fashionable men filled the pave; and between the curb stones whirled one incessant clang of omnibusses, carriages, and other vehicles.

Upon the Battery, pedestrians, singly and in groups, were enjoying the lazy breeze as it wafted along from the bosom of the bay. Quite a "sensation" was created by the starting of the rival steamers, the Worcester and the Massachusetts. They put forth, like high mettled steeds, and those on board them, no doubt, felt as anxious for the success of their favorite boat as e'er a sportsman at Union course for the success of Eclipse or Black Maria.[34]   As they turned the southern point of the Battery, the Worcester was several lengths ahead.

[APRIL 22, 1842]

"We never intend

to mince

matters

. . . .

to stop

for

honeyed words"

Part Two

INSULT TO AMERICAN CITIZENSHIP[1]

I N ANOTHER COLUMN will be found the proceedings of the great meeting held in the Park yesterday afternoon, upon the subject of our New York Public Schools.[2] Some time before the hour of commencement, we noticed squads of men, evidently the lowest class of foreigners, pouring through the gates into the space in front of the City Hall. A solid, compact mass of them crowded close up and around the platform erected for the officers of the meeting. At five o'clock, there were eight or ten thousand persons present, and the foreigners we have mentioned composed about one tenth of that number. The meeting continued about twenty minutes; it was broken up amid great confusion, fighting, and turmoil, proceeding from the gang who had taken possession of the immediate neighborhood of the platform.

Our cheeks are suffused with shame and indignation as we write about this matter, for so gross an insult to our rights as Americans, we have never seen or heard of before. Bands of filthy wretches, whose very touch was offensive to a decent man, drunken loafers; scoundrels whom the police and criminal courts would be ashamed to receive in their walls; coarse, blustering rowdies; blear eyed and bloated offscourings from the stews, blind alleys and rear lanes; disgusting objects bearing the form human, but whom the sow in the mire might almost object to as companions—these were they who broke into the midst of a peaceful body of American citizens—struck and insulted the chosen officers of the assemblage, and with shrieks, loud blasphemy, and howlings in their hideous native tongue, prevented the continuance of the customary routine. We saw Irish priests there—sly, false, deceitful villains—looking on and evidently encouraging the gang who created the tumult. We noticed two or three tavern bullies strike on the head a presiding officer[3]—one of the most aged and respectable men of our city. We beheld the whole body of those officers forced, at length, from their seats, and driven, with jibes and blows, from the stage. And these officers were native Americans—men with grey heads—men known for long years among us as gentlemen of reputation, philanthropy and exalted worth!

And is New York to utter no loud voice of abhorrence toward this

transaction? Is this hypocritical scoundrel Hughes,[4] and his minions, to drill ranks of ignorant and vindictive followers—and send
them forth to act as those wretches acted—and shall no note be taken
of it? It is a blot and an insolent violation of our dearest and most
glorious privileges. The whole city—the whole state—ought to rise
up as one man, and let these jesuitical knaves, and their apt satellites,
know what it is to feel the blast from an injured and outraged country.

We sorrow for out native land. Having no prejudices against foreigners, because they are such, we yet feel that they are becoming
altogether too domineering among us. A portion of them are entirely under the control of that reverend villain, Hughes, who, with
his corrupt and selfish motives, moulds them to suit his will.

It is told us that part of a society known as the Spartan Band[5]
was present in this scandalous attack. We cannot believe it; we cannot think that any men, except the foolish and degraded creatures
who follow in the wake of the Roman priests—would be guilty of
such foul conduct.

We call upon our fellow citizens to teach Hughes and his coadjutors a lesson. Has it come to be, that the American people cannot
gather together for the purpose of an orderly expression of sentiments, without being broken in upon by a gang of foreign outcasts
and bullies, prompted by this fanatical wretch and his slaves? In the
west, where the statute book affords no remedy for outrage, the injured community takes the case into its own hands.

Party spirit has arrived at a dangerous pass, indeed, among us, if
such things can happen—and any political faction be found to continue tampering with the villains who take part in them. Yet party
spirit *has* come to be so all engrossing, that we should not be surprised, if half the papers came out this morning with an account
glossing over the whole transaction.

[MARCH 17, 1842]

THE *AURORA* AND THE SCHOOL QUESTION

A communication was received yesterday at this office, strongly
reprehending the course we have taken upon the public school question. The writer says:

> A personal and political friend of Bishop Hughes, as I am,
> cannot but be amazed at the strictures you have given utterance

to in relation to that gentleman. Are you not afraid that so abusive, malevolent, and groundless an attack will bring a tempest
around your ears that it will be hard to allay?

The Aurora, we imagine, among people who know it, needs no
certificate of its character for courage. We do *not* fear, either the
attacks of those whom, by exposing their wickedness, we have made
enemies of—nor any "tempest" that our conduct may bring down
upon our head. We have nerve enough to face the fire of battle, and
stand by our colors, and peal out the rallying cry to the last, in support of any cause which we sincerely believe to be holy and patriotic.
We dare the utmost malignance and fanaticism can do against us.
Confiding in the might of truth, and doubly cased in the armor of a
"quarrel just," and willing rather to be beaten down in the defense
of right, than raised aloft by advocacy of wrong, we neither fear
this cunning, selfish Hughes, nor any of his wretched gang. Though
we can be lenient to errors, and mistakes that proceed from ignorance or carelessness, we are determined to lay the lash on these wicked men, until they shall feel in their blasted reputations what it is to
receive the vengeance of an outraged people.

But there is one thing in which we *are* a coward. There is one contest that we would approach with fear and trembling—with a
blanched cheek and an unsteady eye—a contest where our courage
would fail us, and where we should very likely turn recreant and
flee. We allude to any attempt to infuse religious sectarianism in the
making of our laws—and poisoning of the constitution with taint
from a meddling priesthood—sowing the discord of superstitious
frenzy so that its fruits ripen in our legislative halls, and flourish in
our civil offices. We have no heart to strive for this.

The Aurora intends to continue the bold and energetic stand it
has taken in this matter—Hughes and his "personal and political
friends" to the contrary notwithstanding. We fancy there are other
people in New York besides the myrmidons of a false villain, who
uses his pontifical robes to cover the blackest, most traitorous heart
in the broad limits of the American republic.

There are generous, brave men—worthy and reputable citizens—
whole souled, spirited, enthusiastic, New Yorkers, whom we meet
almost hourly, and who warmly and heartily approve the steps we
have pursued in this business—and who encourage us to persevere.
So this reverend and hoary hypocrite may count upon *no* retreat on
our part, no backing out, no cessation, no slackening of the guns,
no truce, and no quarter.

[MARCH 18, 1842]

TAMMANY IN TROUBLE

Developments have lately been made which show that the democratic party are in a peck of trouble about the coming charter election. Every idea of duty impels them to oppose a loud mouthed and
insolent faction among them, composed of Catholic foreigners, who
seem determined to rule the party or ruin it. On the other hand, the
leaders fear that if they do as they ought by this faction, a number
of votes will be lost them. It is hardly necessary to add, that these
insolent foreigners are they who follow in the wake of Hughes, the
electioneering priest, in his movements upon the school question.

After being "on the fence" for a long time, the New Era[6] came
out, yesterday, hot and heavy in favor of the Hughes clique. If the
Tammany people wish to damn themselves and their prospects of
success, let them approve this course of the Era. If they wish to pre-
serve the respect of sensible men, and a chance of victory, let them
quickly and decidedly pronounce their condemnation of it.

It is a shame and a disgrace to the glorious name of democracy
—first, that it has such a stupid, vulgar, anti-American newspaper
for its organ, as this rickety New Era, which is only kept afloat by
corporation patronage; and, secondly, that it, the democracy, allows
the Era, to talk in this way about what "the party" are bound to do.

If Slamm wants to go over to the Catholic priests, and aid them
in their patriotic attempts to control the ballot boxes, let him make
tracks with all convenient swiftness; and heaven give them joy of
their distinguished convert. But in the name of American justice, let
not the whole of a great party be thus brought in as servants to a
cabal of foreign jesuits. If Tammany yet retains any of its old
leaven—if it possesses a remnant of the spirit, vigor, and independence of principle, which in times of yore wafted it on to triumph—
if glorious old recollections have not departed from it, and thoughts
of its ancient might abide with it any more—and the memory of how
in times past it has disdained to truckle to threats or bribes, be yet
alive—then let the *true* democratic leaders come out boldly, and dare
to utter the truth. Disdaining to bend, and thinking it scorn to curry
favor with ignorant fanaticism—let them cast themselves on the people's sense of right. And then, with the result in the voices of intelligent American citizens, and under the direction of God, there will
be no such word as fail!

[MARCH 24, 1842]

TAMMANY'S "FAMILY JARS"

No person who has had good opportunities of judging, will deny that the Tammany party *proper*, have a clear and decided majority in the city of New York. The mass of the people are democratic; and they have an ineradicable yearning toward the time honored institution of "the Columbian order."

Late occurrences have shown, however, that there is trouble in the camp. The Catholic interest, resolved to push matters to the verge, has openly proclaimed that the Tammany leaders *must* come out in its favor, or that those foreigners who are under the control of the priests will receive imperative orders to go against the Tammany ticket. Suspended thus between two horns of a dilemma, the commanding officers are at fault. Some of them advocate a bold and manly adherence to right, regardless of consequences; but a number of the weaker vessels think it more wise to tamper with the malcontents, as grown people sometimes play bo-peep with their children.

The New Era, who still sticks to Tammany, like an unwelcome guest, whose room is considered far more valuable than his company—the New Era comes strongly to the advocacy of the Hughes clique. It is hardly necessary for us to remark, that the Era long ago lost caste with the democracy of New York; its vulgarity, its total deficiency of any thing like taste or intellect, or vigor, has made it to be looked upon by a large majority of the democrats as by no means a credit to their cause. Yet, through the means of certain occurrences, which it is unnecessary to define here, the New Era has interwoven itself into Tammany, so that it claims to be their organ; and Tammany, we suppose, feels bound to countenance it, in the same way that a well bred family feel bound to abstain from kicking down stairs a vulgar blackguard, who, being distantly related to them, has gained admittance in their circle, to which he is an eyesore and a botheration.

The democratic party, assuredly, cannot allow themselves to be dictated to by an insolent faction, led on by Romish priests. The voice of the New Era is by no means the voice of the democracy; as reasonable would it be to consider that the dullest "supe" employed at the Park theatre represents the capacities of the American stage.

[MARCH 26, 1842]

ORGANS OF DEMOCRACY

It is useless to conceal the fact that the democratic party in New York labor under the disadvantage of having no publication really creditable to them, and really calculated to further their interests. At the present time, the Post, Standard, and New Era,[7] are all at loggerheads. The rock on which they split is the school question; the Standard being plumply in favor of the existing system—the Post also evidently opposed to a change, yet fearful to come out openly —the Era violently arrayed on the side of Hughes and the Catholic priests.

The plain truth of the matter is, it is only by the most strenuous exertions that the New Era has permission to keep out its flag as the organ of Tammany Hall. A large majority of the democratic leaders do not hesitate to express their contempt and dissatisfaction with the Era. They are openly in favor of lopping off from any connection with that stupid print. In this exigency the Era knows that by taking up cudgels for the defence of the Catholic interest, it will have that interest disciplined to its support, as a kind of forlorn hope. The Era undoubtedly thinks, too, that the Tammany leaders will not have the fearlessness decidedly to repudiate the move it has taken—for fear of losing the votes of those under the control of the priests. It remains to be seen whether the whole democratic party are to be led by the nose, by this manoeuvre of a clique of jesuits, and a paper which thus stabs the vitals of the party for the chance of a little advantage to itself.

Not a word has been said by the Era, about the nomination of Robert H. Morris[8] as mayor. The Hughes faction, no doubt, are opposed to that nomination. For our own part, we do not think the city could select a more worthy man than he who at present occupies the mayoralty. He has all the qualifications of experience, ability, and character, that are necessary. As far as we have any preference, therefore, at present, we hope Morris will win the race.

It is wonderful that the democrats do not take summary steps in this business. It is an insult and a disgrace to the party, that a journal presuming to be their organ should thus barter away their honor, and marshall itself under the dictation of a selfish clique of *foreigners.*

The Tammany party want, here in New York, a newspaper bold, manly, able, and *American* in its tenor; a newspaper vigorous and original and fresh. Until they have such a one, the organs at present recognized as theirs, will be no better than dead weight to them.[9]

[MARCH 29, 1842]

DEFINING "OUR POSITION"[10]

From one of the best known and most respectable citizens of New York—one who, as formerly occupant of a high official station under the general government, and distinguished no less for his abilities in literature and science, has identified himself with the first men of the western world—we yesterday received a note somewhat taking us to task for the course this paper has lately pursued, and offering certain suggestions for our future conduct. Were we permitted to give the name of our correspondent, our readers would perceive with what propriety we can depart in this instance from our general course, and "give explanations." The writer of the letter says:—

> "Notwithstanding that I, in common with nearly all whom I have conversed with upon the matter, cannot deny the evidently patriotic motives, the eloquence, and the unflinching courage, which characterise your attacks on what you have enmity toward —yet there appears a kind of vindictiveness, a want of charity, a disposition to ultraism, which must be highly offensive to persons of correct views. You have loaded those whom you dislike with abuse and opprobrium to a degree that I do not recollect ever to have seen equalled before; the fiercest invective, and the hottest hate can hardly lead you farther than you have already gone. I question whether the English language affords superlatives more superlative than you have piled on, mountain high, upon the heads of certain individuals whose conduct you disapprove.
>
> "And most decidedly do I condemn your stand against FOR-EIGNERS. That body, like all that is human, have their demerits, undoubtedly; but it is too late in the day to get up a crusade against them. You might as well deprive the tree of its sap, as America of its influx of foreign emigrants."

Our reply to the above will be very brief. And we shall answer first, that which our respected correspondent has complained of last. The motives of the Aurora, in some of its recent steps, have been much misunderstood. We have no antipathy or bigotted ill will to *foreigners.* God forbid! Our love is capacious enough, and our arms wide enough, to encircle all men, whether they have birth in our glorious republic, the monarchies of Europe, or the hot deserts of Africa—whatever be their origin or their native land. Our mind is not one of that narrow description which confines its good will by a shore or a boundary line; we look upon all human beings as brethren, entitled all to our regard, our good offices, the protection of government, and the enjoyment of freedom.

Yet we cannot shut our eyes to the painful truth that this nation— all vigorous in the bloom of youth, and, like youth, susceptible to a lasting stamp from chance impressions—is in danger of being deterred from a proud and lofty path, by influences of an anti-American tendency spread through its width and breadth, and made more plenty by every packet and steam ship that arrives in our docks from abroad. We possess in this republic the advantages and the capacities, for evolving the Great Problem—the problem of how far Man, the masterpiece of cunningest Omniscience, can have his nature perfected by himself, and can be trusted to govern himself. We possess the chance of spreading to the gaze of the world, the glorious spectacle of a continent peopled by *freemen*—freemen, not as those of vaunted Rome, and voluptuous Venice—not free in grades—but freemen in a reality far beyond even what our nation now enjoys. We would that all the taint of time defiled custom—all the poisonous atmosphere of European philosophy—all the fallacious glitter of a literature which, being under the patronage of courts and princes and haughty church, is not fitted for our beloved America—all the aristocratic nations, interwoven so closely with social customs, as to be almost ineradicable—we would that all this might have no sway in the land. These things are not for such as we. A higher and holier destiny, a more worthy mission, we sincerely hope, belongs to us.

And now the public can see what kind of *Americanism* will characterise the *Aurora*. We glory in such principles; we would rather use our strength in diffusing them, than, like some of our contemporaries, reap the harvest of basely pandering to error, and feeding vanity. There are among the conductors of our newspapers too many

"dastard sycophants and jesters—
Reptiles who lay their bellies in the dust,
Before the frown of majesty."

He who chalks out the campaign for the *Aurora*, is not of them.

Our correspondent also takes it ill that some of our editorials show "the fiercest invective, and the hottest hate." It would be affectation, were we to pretend not to understand what are the instances alluded to. We are well aware that we used strong language; we *meant* to. Though professing to be by no means of excitable temperment—we are ever roused to the utmost, by any such conduct as this of the dastardly Hughes, and his kindred fanatical demagogues. The farthest stretch of condemnation cannot go too far against any proceedings which put in jeopardy the soundness and purity of the elective franchise.

We never *intend* to mince matters—to stop for honeyed words—to crust the wholesome dose we administer, with sugar—to be polite unto filthy vice—to stand on ceremony with a traitor—or treat a scoundrel with dainty punctilio.

[MARCH 30, 1842]

TAMMANY MEETING LAST NIGHT

A great gathering of the Democracy convened at Tammany Hall last evening. John I. Morgan was chosen chairman, and a long string of resolutions was passed, expressing nothing particular—and taking care most ingeniously not to touch any of the sore points which are at present existing upon the "body politic."

Messrs. Field,[11] Vanderpocl,[12] Sedgwick,[13] and Morrell,[14] addressed the assemblage and spurred them on to do their best in the coming contest. They endeavored to pour as much oil as possible upon the waters; and from the fact that the Irish present very condescendingly permitted themselves to refrain from hissing, or breaking up the affair in a row—we presume the speakers were successful.

We are confident, however, that they have only scotched the snake, not killed it. Hughes and his faction are *determined* to have decided friendship or war to the knife. They are insolent, overbearing, and not to be cajoled. They have nominated a separate ticket,[15] and will undoubtedly go for it, heart and soul.

Tammany puts on a smiling face, meantime—but no one with sharp eyes, but can see that she is in a pack of trouble. That wretched hack, the New Era, does its best to widen the breach still more. It has, to a degree, identified the democrats with the movements of the Catholic priests—those hired fomenters of discord, and assassins of union.

We beseech the democratic party, in this matter, to take a stand worthy of their professed principles. As they love the memory of Washington—as they adhere to the teachings of Jefferson—as they prize the safety, present and future, of our beloved republic—we implore them to speak out against the machinations of these reverend demagogues.

What is the gain of an alderman or a mayor, or the whole city ticket, to the establishing of a precedent for the introduction of sectarianism in our politics? No man can calculate the danger—no eye can look far enough ahead to perceive the horrors that may ensue from following out this precedent.

Again we entreat that portion, (and it is a large portion) of the democracy, who condemn the policy of the Hughes clique, and their convenient pimp, the New Era, to stand firm and falter not.

One thing is certain—the steps taken by the conductors of the Era, have been so grossly insulting to their party, so uncalled for, so scandalous to the dignity of American citizenship—that the Era may expect, ere three months have passed away, either to be formally read out of meeting, or else allowed to sink quietly in the grave of newspapers lost from earth—scorned by every man, and regretted far more by Tammany's foes than Tammany itself.

[APRIL 6, 1842]

DISSENSIONS OF TAMMANY

From authentic sources we are assured that there will before long be a grand flare up in Tammany. We "shouldn't wonder" at all. The fanning of flames of discord, and the attempts of a moiety to rule or ruin, and the blind adherence of another moiety to a course which will evidently lead to overthrow—all these operate in such a manner as to make an open rupture inevitable.

For a long series of years, the democratic nominations have depended largely for their success upon the votes of adopted citizens. A large portion of this body is now in open rebellion. It has been induced to think itself of great importance — to consider its value as far higher than it really is. Caresses have been bestowed upon these people, and so much has from time to time been yielded to their whims—that they imagine *nothing* must be denied them. The democratic candidate for re-election to the mayoralty may expect no votes from the adopted citizens. Morris himself does not expect any. They are open and loud in their determination to go strong against him.

The New Era cannot *govern* Tammany. Joined with the Catholic interest, and both together holding power over several hundred ballots—they can *threaten* her; but she has too much of her ancient spirit left to yield to fear. The most respectable and intelligent portion of the democrats are decided in their resolution to love Rome more than Caesar.

It is but a short while ago, that a project was formed by a number of the leading democrats of New York to establish a paper to supersede the Era. Whether the Era people promised amendment, or whether from pity to its certain dissolution, we know not; but the project was never carried through. At various times a number of other attempts have been made to furnish Tammany with a respectable newspaper. And though these attempts were abortive, they serve to show, plainly enough, the dissatisfaction and contempt with which the party themselves look upon their accredited organ.

The democratic party is far from *unfriendly* to foreigners. While the federalists of former times, and "National Republicans" of a later date, have obstinately persisted in refusing to acknowledge the claims of adopted citizens to the elective franchise, Tammany has stood forth, their bold and eloquent champion. And this has been because democracy, in its true practice, acknowledges the great universality of rights, and all men's claims to the blessings of government.

But Tammany will *never* be ruled by a clique of ignorant demagogues and foreign priests. Let the dissevering of the old bond of union come as quick as it may, (and that it *must* come in a very few weeks, no one can doubt,) the democratic party cannot, *will not* yield their dignity as American citizens, their rights as freemen, and their love of country as republicans and patriots. Hughes and the New Era may embroil the party—but they will never be allowed to tyrannise over it.

[APRIL 1, 1842]

THE MASK THROWN OFF

At last, the Catholics have put away disguise, and openly told us what their course is to be. We thank them for it. We shall now be able to meet them in open combat, and not fight as heretofore with foes who battle in the Indian method, by stratagem, and each man hid behind a stump or a bush. At the great meeting of the Hughes faction, in St. John's Hall, last Monday evening, they adopted a resolve, that if the Senate pass Maclay's school bill, O'Connor, the "Independent Democratic Republican" candidate for Mayor will be withdrawn—if not, not. The same threat is reiterated by a stupid, wishy washy Catholic paper, started a few days since somewhere hereabouts; and, moreover, it is a matter of town talk.

Will the democracy yield? Shall a gang of false and villainous priests, whose despicable souls never generate any aspiration beyond their own narrow and horrible and beastly superstition—shall these dregs of foreign filth—refuse of convents—scullions from Austrian monasteries—be permitted thus to dictate what Tammany *must* do?

The bulwark of truth—the "unterrified democracy," ruled by a tattered, coarse, unshaven, filthy, Irish rabble! Americans, high in reputation, degrading themselves worse than the slavish nobles who of old kissed the toe of the triple crowned? *They* knelt to the Pope himself; *Americans*, to the abjectest menials of the Pope.

We know there are large numbers of democrats to whom this is a bitter pill—but they think it must be swallowed to insure their candidates success. In order, then, that a few paltry offices may be filled by "our party," they are content to be thus servile!

But we *cannot* think the democratic voters will be led by the nose in this manner. Let them act as *men*—come out, as American patriots, and defy the priest Hughes to do his worst. He and his allowed to sway political elections?

> "Rather than so, come fate into the list,
> And champion me to th' utterance."[16]

It were better that all should be lost, than such a precedent established. The foreign riffraff once yielded to in this case, and there will be no end to their demands and their insolence. Now is the crisis. If Tammany bends, she breaks. Democracy, instead of remaining a term of honor—will be but another word to signify the rule of hypocritical monks, reverend traitors who steal the livery of the court of heaven to serve the devil in.

[APRIL 7, 1842]

[BLACK-HEARTED DECEIT]

On Saturday night, the news arrived that Maclay's school bill, as amended, had passed the Senate, 13 to 12. Mr. Varian[17] voted against it; Scott[18] dodged the question, and absented himself.

At last, then, the Rubicon is crossed. The machinations and insolent threats of the Hughes clique have had their effect. We feel almost too shocked, too shamed at the very name of New York legislative honor, to give full utterance to our thoughts upon this matter. We were in hopes that there were some remnants of spirit in the bosoms of the democratic leaders at Albany—remnants sufficiently strong in degree to prevent the passage of this scandalous enactment—this statute for the fostering and teaching of Catholic superstition!

Mr. Varian deserves honor; though we have not the pleasure of personal acquaintance with him, it will be his fault, if, at the first opportunity, we do not take him warmly by the hand, and express how deeply he has impressed us with respect for his patriotism, and his brave devotion to principle.

As to this Scott, he deserves to be kicked from the presence of every man pretending to decency. He is not only an unprincipled political scoundrel, but has evinced himself to be low, mean, and contemptible in his every disposition. He had not courage to come out openly in favor of the Hughes clique, but takes this back stairs, half hid method of pandering to their interests. He is almost a blot to mention in the pages of a respectable newspaper!

Never was there a darker, more treacherous, despicable, and selfish game than that played, in this business, by a cabal among the leaders of Tammany—a cabal which, while it is a minority of Tammany itself, is sufficiently artful to send out its edicts as coming from the whole party. We *know* it to be the case, that when the Hughes clique threatened Tammany with defection unless the school bill passed, a delegation was sent up to Albany, with imperative commands to Scott, Varian, and all the rest who would let themselves be commanded, to vote for the bill. The delegation returned without attaining the object of their mission. Last Thursday, the aspect of the political horizon becoming still more gloomy, a second delegation was despatched, with orders to spare nothing, menace, entreaty, or expostulation, for the purpose of whipping the obstinate senators into the traces. This second embassy was successful, inasmuch as it seems that Scott was persuaded to absent himself, and let the bill go by means of that absence.

And these persons call themselves men of *principle!* Why, from beginning to end, the course of the democratic party—that portion of it who have bent to the dictation of the Austrian jesuits, and their associate the New Era, appears one continued string of trickery, black hearted deceit, and corrupt manoeuvring. Not only has the very name of democrat been made a jeer and hiss; not only have the legislative votes been a matter of traffic, for the wretchedest partizan purpose; not only have principles been thrust aside, and the dearest interest of the city bartered to obtain support from the low Irish; but all has been done *openly*, done without even a decent veil to cover its nakedness. The well being of our children yields to the commands of foreign renegades. The "unterrified democracy" crouches at the feet of papal dictation, and is routed by a gathering of foreign scum.

It is now too late to do any thing in tomorrow's election, to show the unprincipled men who have engaged in this measure, what utter disgust is felt toward the course pursued by them. Let all, however, do what can be done. Let every New Yorker, who feels how gross has been the conduct of both parties in this business, stay away from the polls and vote for neither ticket. If the riffraff, Hughes, and that despicable press, the New Era, are to rule the city, let it be not through the means of votes from men who have any American feeling.

We repeat it, let every person who does not belong to and is not friendly to the Catholic interest, stay away from the polls, and vote for neither party. And especially let those democrats, (and we feel confident we speak to no small number,) who blush for the course pursued by their party in this business give it not the countenance of their suffrage.

[APRIL 11, 1842]

TOMORROW

The great political dance is to be led off tomorrow. In consequence of the "Independent Democratic Republican" candidate for mayor having withdrawn, Morris will probably receive the votes of many of the Catholics. We question, however, whether a much larger number of his own party will not remain away from the polls—disgusted with the total want of principle which has characterised the Tammany leaders in their bargaining with the Catholics. Every democrat, certainly, who is not of the Hughes clique, or who does not think that "expediency" is palliation enough for basely trucking to reverend insolence will withhold his support from the whole ticket, from mayor down to collector.

There is still a good deal of discord among the rival factions. Each seeks to embarrass the other. And about the flimsiest of all the manoeuvres "got up" for that purpose, is the late attempt to nominate a Tyler whig for the mayoralty. A new paper, the Arena,[19] and the democratic New Era, have been laying their heads together to do something that shall distract the whigs, and therefore advantage the democrats. The Arena, it seems, has taken upon itself to claim to be considered as a "Tyler organ"; and the New Era affects to speak of it as such.

Through the help of the conductors of those papers, and a few other bastard democrats, the Washington Hall meeting was convened, and James Monroe nominated. The plain truth is, that *no* whigs (except false ones—as false to the whig party, as their associates are to *theirs*) were engaged in the movement. It was a bare faced, contemptible trick—worthy of its parentage on both sides. If any Whig, therefore, is gulled by this stupid piece of bungling deception, he may thank his own ignorance and credulity.

The democratic party wants regenerating. If it wishes to keep any of its former purity, strength, and power, it will have to kick out several time serving unprincipled men, who have within the past few years poisoned its counsels, and dishonored its reputation.

[APRIL 11, 1842]

[GROSS POLITICAL CHICANERY]

It is a fearful thing that our country has arrived at a pass where parties will openly sell their influence to cabals, for the votes of the cabals. The Tammany papers may try to gloss over the scandalous bargaining between their party and the Hughes faction; but it is plainly the most complete piece of political chicanery that ever disgraced the annals of the land. The Irish "Independent Democrats" threatened—and Tammany plucked up spirit enough, at first, to resist. The Irish threatened a second time, and with double fierceness; and Tammany bowed her neck to the very dust.

We are sure that there *must* be such men as *American* democrats in Tammany. Where were they while this abominable game was going on? Where was their patriotism—their hatred of interweaving priestcraft with politics—their love of liberty undefiled—and their care for the interests of their children?

That they could tamely have stood by, and consented to this thing —for God's love we could hardly believe. They must have been caught napping; the enemy must have entered the citadel in the dark.

And now only one thing remains. Let them show that paltry partizanship has not deadened every remnant of love of country. Let them—we beseech them as *American republicans*—let them not cast away self respect and self rights at the command of the minions of foreign convents, and the menaces of an Irish riffraff. Every suffrage given by a democrat for the Tammany ticket is so much to aid the behests of the Hughes clique.

There is no candidate in the field who has the least claim upon a true American voter. In particular, let those men who have so anxiously sought Catholic patronage, that they have given up every thing to Catholic dictation—let them, we say, rest exclusively on Catholic support. It certainly is not becoming for honorable democrats, to countenance them. A defeat of the Tammany ticket might teach the Tammany leaders a wholesome lesson.

We call, then, upon all *American* hearts to join in a determination to abstain from supporting the so called democratic ticket.[20] We ask this, "not that we love Cæsar less, but that we love Rome more." We love (why should we conceal it?) we love the name of democrat. It has been our pride and glory to keep the title untarnished, as we inherited it from those who carried the then opprobrious term amid the stormy political tempests of Jefferson's day. But we cannot flatter the base, and fawn to hypocrisy, and wriggle, and *lie*, for the interests of any petty clique. True democracy requires such things of no man for any purpose.

Today, the opportunity will be presented for democrats to show whether they, as individuals, are content to be lickspittles to Austrian monks, and filthy foreign vagabonds. If they cannot say NO! let them at least not say YES!

[APRIL 12, 1842]

LAST EVENING

The first patterings of the tempest—the *reveille*—the portents of the coming battle—were to be seen and heard in all directions last evening. Between five and six o'clock, a strange, good humored, heterogeneous mass of young and old, gentlemen and loafers, began to congregate in the Park; and though professedly the call was for a "Tyler meeting," we question whether nineteen twentieths were not known friends either to Clay or to "regular democratic nominations." About six o'clock, we stepped over in front of the City Hall to see what was going on. As near as we could judge, two thousand people were present—and every one, apparently, in a huge good humor, joking, and merry without restraint. Col Hamilton,[21] up on the steps, backed against one of the marble columns, was reading from a MS. paper, though we should imagine only those in his immediate vicinity could have heard him. Now and then, the people at his left would swing their hats, and cry "Hurrah for Clay!" Then those at the right would start a "Hurrah for Van Buren!" As soon as the noise subsided, some enthusiastic fellow down in the crowd would call "Three cheers for Phoenix!"[22] which was just as surely wound up by "Three cheers for Bob Morris!"[23] All this time, Col. Hamilton kept reading on, though it was like talking to the stormy waves.

We believe there were no fights, or rows; but the whole of this amusing conglomeration of idlers allowed each other to hurrah for just whoever he blessed please. Can it be that the Herald, or any other print, will come out this morning with an attempt to continue the gag of a "Tyler meeting?" The whole of this manoeuvre is about as bungling and poor worked a game as we ever saw played. Its very parentage is ashamed of it.

At night, the great transparency in front of Tammany was all lit, and the gas touched up in the big room. Just after eight o'clock, when we edged our entrance in the room, James M. Smith was holding forth upon the rostrum, and from what we heard of his remarks we should set them down as mere common place stuff, intended to "tickle the ears of the groundlings." He soft soaped the foreigners present; and they, as in duty bound, applauded him loudly. How long will Tammany be under leading strings to fifth rate pettifoggers, and wrangling limbs of the laws?

When Smith concluded, the great Kinderhook roarer[24] came forward. Had we not seen the learned gentleman in times bygone, we should certainly have despatched some one post haste after a physician; for such spasmodic contortions—such horrible and ghastly grimaces—such terrible evidences of bad digestion, and the want of Sherman's lozenges[25]—it made us quite uncomfortable to behold. Is it true that this Vanderpoel pretends to be a *gentleman?* Such low, vulgar scurrility—such beastly coarseness—such claptrap, stale trash—such gross egotism, and such pandering to the worst prejudices of the Irish, whom it seemed his peculiar desire to make his hail fellows well met—our ears were never before disgusted with; and we cannot but be solemnly impressed with the idea that Fortune has made a great mistake in placing this overgrown lubber among the society of decent men. He said he was "half an Irishman" himself. We presume respectable Americans would not grieve much were he "whole hog" Irish.

In the course of the evening, we stepped into several of the ward meetings—one at Tom Riley's, one at Dunn's, and one at the Marion House, in West Broadway. They seemed to be slim affairs all round —very little enthusiasm, and very little confidence of success in either party.

To all appearances, there is no certainty for either ticket. The Morris candidates flatter themselves with an easy victory, from their having gained the Catholic interest back to their support. Large masses, however, of those who would have voted for them, will not do so, since the open identification of the Tammany ticket with the Hughes faction.

Ward processions, with banners and music, paraded the streets until midnight, and after.

[APRIL 12, 1842]

[A SMALL POTATO ARNOLD]

"When the list of names was called over to record the votes, Judge Scott, who but half an hour before *had voted against order-*

ing the bill to a third reading, had skulked. This may seem strange but when I tell you that in the interval between the last vote of Judge Scott and the calling of his name on the final passage, *John Van Buren* had his honor cornered in the ante room the whole time, you will cease to wonder."

So says the Tribune of yesterday morning.

We have, in our years, seen examples of slippery, cowardly, sordid politicians—but this Scott out Herods Herod. Not one iota of manliness, of honesty, or of patriotism, appears to reside in his character. The very clique whom he has pandered, to, cannot but look upon him with contempt. His villainy is perpetrated in such a dissembling, timid, consciously guilty manner that he sinks below the regard even of his kindred rascals. They *can* call him "fool, as well as villain."

In yesterday's Standard this small potato Arnold attempts to screen himself by a humdrum excuse about his bargaining with a fellow senator to stay away, jointly with himself, and so balance each other. And this in the face of the notorious fact that he, Scott, was sent for, (being but a short distance off,) and informed that the vote was to be taken, *and refused to come!* Did ever a man, pretending to be a man, utter such a scandalous lie? He *knew* the bill was to come up—was already up. He had not intrepidity enough to act as became an honorable treasurer of the people's rights—he had not strength of mind enough to resist the seductive tones of the *eloquent* sap head, who, we are told in the first paragraph above, was at his elbow—he had not even that redeeming spark of scoundrelism, its boldness—he childishly vacillated between the hope of future fat office from the patronage of his priestly commanders, and the fear of covering himself with infamy from backing out of his old professions—and so he *skulked way!* It would be an insult to the memory of Judas to say that the twain resemble each other.

Were it possible for this dastardly creature to render his reputation any more black, his letter to the Standard, which we have spoken of, might do it. He has posted himself to the whole city as an unprincipled *liar!*

If ever any scoundrel deserved a coat of tar and feathers, this base senator is the one. And yet it would defile the fingers of an honest citizen to touch him. Let his punishment be the contempt, scorn, and frowns of the people; and the consciousness in his own mind that though his station shields him, he *deserves* to be kicked by every one of his constitutents.

[APRIL 12, 1842]

RESULT OF THE ELECTION

As our readers will perceive by tables in another part of today's paper—Robert H. Morris is re-elected mayor of the city. His majority cannot be less than two thousand. The democratic ticket is successful in the Fourth and Seventh wards, which have hitherto gone for the whigs; and lost in the Sixth positively—and possibly the Eighth, Sixteenth, and Twelfth, and a slight chance also of the Fourteenth. If all these latter are defective—which is barely possible—the whigs will have a majority in the common council; if not, not.

Though Morris himself is a good officer and worthy man, we did not hesitate in opposing him and his whole ticket; as we should do the same thing, under like circumstances, again. No merit is there, to our taste, in gaining success through base truckling to a conglomeration of foreign vagabonds and rowdies. We would rather the whole Tammany ticket had gone by the board, than that the Catholic priests should in this manner, have an example of their power, to which to point back, and say, in future—Behold what might we have to sway your elections to one side or the other—behold and tremble!

Is it not a pleasant spectacle for an American to look upon? The greatest and most popular of the parties of the republic, bending to the very feet of the dictation of a rude, ignorant rabble! American citizens—good men and true—insolently browbeaten by a minority of foreign bullies; our own people, born and brought up among us, forced to stand aside, and humbly doff their hats, like menials in the presence of their masters!

Has it come to be, that *Irishman* is a better title to office, here, than *American?* When the coarse, illiterate Kinderhook roarer proclaimed himself to be "half Irish," in Tammany Hall, night before last, there arose cheer after cheer, peal after peal, shaking the very ground, and almost deafening the hearer; had he called himself merely *American,* he would have been listened to with apathy.

For our own part, we confess that while our philanthropy is wide enough to take in all nations, grades, and sects, the love nearest and closest to our heart is reserved for *our own beloved republic, and for our free born American citizens.*

The Irish will now probably be ten times more insolent than ever. Yet is the scale turning—and that with no small rapidity. Hundreds and hundreds of democrats yesterday, reflecting on the course pursued in this business, and viewing the conduct of the foreigners during the day, were open in their expressions of disgust and dissatisfaction with themselves for not having promptly nipped the matter in the bud.

P. S.—The actual political complexion of the Common Council was not known for certain when we went to press, although at 2 o'clock the probability, was that the whigs had elected their aldermen and assistants in the 1st, 2d, 3d, 4th, 5th, 6th, 8th, 12th, 14th, 15th and 16th wards—ten of the 17 wards.

[APRIL 13, 1842]

INCIDENTS OF LAST NIGHT

The democratic head quarters, Tammany Hall, and the whig headquarters, National Hall, were filled with their respective partizans, anxious to hear the returns from the various wards, and to obtain a knowledge of the result of the contest.

During the latter part of the day there had been a great row down in the neighborhood of the Tombs, between some squads of Irish, and a number of Americans, whom they insulted grossly. The Irish had armed themselves with billets of wood, and in the course of their triumphal passage through the streets, it seemed they met with some spirited young fellows[26] who had no great taste for submitting to their abuse and domineering bravado. The consequence was that there was a general battle. The bog trotters, were completely routed, and many of them, with a portion of their assailants, captured by the police.

About 9 o'clock we stepped in at Tammany Hall, where we found the crowd great, and the passages and walks in front filled with an immense mass of people—some attracted by curiosity, but most of them anxious to hear the returns, as they were brought in by emissaries from the wards. Edging our way with infinite difficulty, we managed at last to effect an entrance into the great room. We will not pretend to criticise the *speaking* we heard during our five minutes' stay; it was beneath the depth of deepness. At intervals, the presiding officer would read off the majorities, as he received them at the hands of the people just arrived from the polls.

It took us nearly half an hour to squeeze ourself down stairs and out in the street again. In the course of the evening, we stepped up to National Hall, but meeting an immense current flowing outward from the door, and being informed by a friend whom we recognized, that "the people there were all *sick,* and were going home for the night," we did not think it judicious to attempt an entrance.

Coming homeward, squads of men were at every corner, and along on the curbstones, holding animated discussion upon the result of the day's contest, and the causes of the result. As near as we could judge from their remarks, the democrats were far from satisfied with themselves and the course they had pursued. They felt, as they ought, like people who had been guilty of something by no means creditable to their manliness.

There was no rejoicing during the evening, at Tammany—none of the usual enthusiasm—none of joyous gratulation, with which they are wont to greet one another in times of victory. In fact never have we beheld such evidences of conscious wrong performed. All the pleasure of their triumph was deadened by their remembrance of the means through which it had been obtained.

In the course of the evening, some of the windows of the priest Hughes' residence were broken by brickbats. Had it been the reverend hypocrite's head, instead of his windows, we could hardly find it in our soul to be sorrowful.

There were rumors, late at night, that two or three persons had been seriously, perhaps fatally injured in the melee. It is impossible, however, to tell, to any degree of certainty, whether they are correct.

                              *   *   *

Since writing the above, we hear from our windows at this moment (between 12 and 1 o'clock, morning) the sounds of martial array in the Park. Two companies of the Washington Greys, on horseback, are defiling through the large gates, into Chatham street, and so up the Bowery. Strong fears are entertained that there will be disturbances before daylight. The police force, and the military, we are informed by one of our reporters, just from the mayor's office, will be kept on duty all night.

The indignation of large numbers of our citizens is roused to a pitch altogether ungovernable, against the insults and absolute trampling upon American citizenship, by the Catholics and the ignorant Irish. What conduct this indignation will exhibit itself in, it is impossible to tell. Hughes' house is much injured; and in all likelihood the cathedrals would have been attacked and sacked, if the people had not been deterred by the military.

In view of the transactions of the past two weeks, who can wonder that such things are acted as we record in the last two or three paragraphs?

[APRIL 13, 1842]

[A HIGHER DEVOTION THAN PARTY]

According to the best authenticated returns, last evening, our read-ers will perceive that while Morris gains his election by handsome majorities, the whigs have obtained a decided preponderance in the Common Council. It is well.

We were never brought up to rejoice at the defeat of democratic candidates. Yet our republican schooling has taught us that there are duties far higher and holier than devotion to the local interests of party. There are times, too, when overthrow is better than con-quest. A sudden pulling of the reins, though it thrills through the structure of the body politic with startling shock, may teach no un-needed lesson.

Tammany is vanquished. For it is little that the mere presiding officer of the city is of her side, while the essentials of power reside with her antagonists.

Yet is the moral a wholesome one—one that, viewed in the proper light, may impress upon the minds of men a great truth. When the representatives of St. John's Hall clique insolently endeavored to browbeat the democrats into submission, the latter should have nobly entrenched themselves upon the rock of principle, and bidden defi-ance to the storm. But as Tammany allowed herself to be *driven,* she has little right to grieve when she reaps the harvest of her folly. The gods look with no favor on men who evince a want of confidence in the intrinsic justice of their own cause. Had Tammany stood forth with an honorable reliance on her principles and her *countrymen,* she would in all probability have succeeded. And even if defeated, as now she is, the satisfaction would be hers, of having done nothing to deserve defeat. As it is, she is not only defeated, but dishonored.

[APRIL 14, 1842]

PLOTS OF THE JESUITS!

We went down, yesterday afternoon, to the scene of the grand fight, on Tuesday, between the Irish and the Spartans. The windows and blinds were completely smashed. In the bar room, we noticed several heaps of bricks, and other missiles, carefully preserved in such a manner as to be evidences of the devestation. But singularly enough, there were numerous objects totally uninjured, (we were in-formed that all was just as it was left by the rioters,) in positions, right through which it was absolutely certain the missiles must have projected, in order to reach the places where they lay.

There were drinking glasses, for instance, behind which we beheld stones and billets of wood, that by some mysterious process, had been sent directly through the said glasses, without injuring them in the least. We cannot minutely describe the whole appearance of the room; but we question whether any of the speculators were not filled with marvel as to how certain pieces of furniture kept whole, in the positions they then occupied.

That there was a great row nobody doubts. But that there was any danger to the inspectors or to the safety of the ballot boxes is very questionable. And there appeared yesterday such a studied desire to make as much as possible of the affair—such a careful anxiety to impress every looker on with an opinion that far more had been done than was really done—so much of misery put on for the occasion, in the entire spectacle—that we shouldn't wonder if the Catholics themselves started the whole rumpus, merely to generate sympathy for their cause, and to make capital of. These jesuits understand how to play their cards as well as the other fellow.

We do not mean to assert that the damage and disturbance were not from the antagonists of the Irish, in some instances. No one who saw the bloody heads and the bruised limbs that the police office, on Tuesday night, swarmed with, but must have known that the foreign rowdies met with a warm reception from some quarter or other. But we honestly believe that the smashing of the priest Hughes' windows, and much of the damage done at the Sixth Ward Hotel, came directly at the instance of the Catholics themselves.

The bare faced farce at Dunn's, and an impartial consideration of the whole matter, justify any man in arriving at this opinion.

[APRIL 14, 1842]

THE LATE RIOTS[27]

A very incorrect idea has gone abroad with respect to the degree of guilt attributable to certain parties in the riots of last Tuesday. We have carefully gleaned from authentic sources and from eye witnesses, a history of the whole affair, which may be relied on as giving the right view of the case.

About the middle of the afternoon, a squad of tipsy fellows, Yankee Sullivan, Ford, and several Spartans, came down the Bowery, followed by a long string of boys, and some larger idlers, attracted probably, by the expectation of seeing "fun." They shaped their course for the Sixth Ward Hotel, and when arrived there, amused themselves with getting into a squabble with some Irishmen, (one party as much to blame as the other,) whom they thrashed, and then allowed to escape. After this, Yankee Sullivan and the Spartans strolled off in another direction, little thinking of the events that were going to follow.

In the meantime, the exasperated Irish retreated to their homes and neighborhoods, gathered over a hundred of their countrymen, armed with blugeons, sticks of cordwood, &c., and returned to the field of their late rout. Finding the victors gone, they marched up and down Centre street, wreaking vengeance on every person whose appearance or conduct they took a fancy to dislike. No one dared oppose them. Their shouts and howls were perfectly terrific; and we are told the residents in that quarter of the town expected every second to see devastation commence upon their dwellings and their families.

Things went on in this way for a couple of hours, when the Spartans, hearing, in some distant part of the city, of what was being transacted, and, no doubt, feeling ripe for a little mischief, returned and showed signs of fight. The Irish drew up a threatening front; but so indignant were the Americans who had been witnessing the outrageous insolence of these foreign rowdies, that they joined with the Spartans; and both turning heartily to, the enemy was completely demolished a second time.

The Irish fled, and entrenching themselves in the houses in the neighborhood, still kept up the fight by throwing down stones, blocks, and other missiles upon the heads of their pursuers. The Spartans, determined to make the lesson a complete one, burst in the doors, dragged out their antagonists, and cracked their heads.

Much sympathy has been thrown away upon the defeated party. The fact is, they brought on their punishment by their own bravado and by themselves being the attackers. We have no disposition to palliate rows or rowdies—but as far as the Spartans and the other American citizens were concerned in the affair, we can see nothing in their conduct to condemn.

[APRIL 15, 1842]

THE CATHOLIC ROWS NOT ENDED

Every evening since Tuesday last, the upper part of Mulberry street, and all the thoroughfares in the neighborhood of St. Patrick's Cathedral, have been in one continued uproar, from the setting in of night until day dawn. The Irish, it seems, are possessed of the idea that their church is to be attacked; and the wicked priests do all they can to fan the flame. Patrols and squads of angry men, jabbering in their peculiar brogue, pass along the walks every few minutes. Numbers of the most enthusiastic sleep all night in the cathedral, and keep up a sentry guard, as garrisons do when invested by the enemy. In the day time, the serpent tongues of their reverend commanders are busied from house to house, in pouring poison into the ears of their credulous flock. They know well enough that the results they profess to fear are ridiculous and utterly out of the question; but it suits their malignant natures best to see as much strife and dissension as possible.

At midnight between Thursday and yesterday, a man went up Mulberry street and the cross streets thereabout, knocking at the doors of the houses tenanted by Irish, with an axe, and calling upon them to arouse, and come forth. Before long, as many as two hundred were out, and arranged in rude, military style—most of them carrying their "own peculiar," the shelalah; and thirty or forty who occupied the front ranks, armed with loaded guns. The whole livelong night they marched to and fro, making darkness hideous with their howlings and their exhibitions of warlike ferocity. The inhabitants of the neighborhood were kept up till morning, without sleep, in very fear that the next moment might bring devastation and bloodshed to their bedsides. A gentleman, resident in Mulberry street, who was at our office yesterday, informed us that his wife was lying ill, and that in consequence of the terror caused by the conduct of these brutal savages, her sickness is very likely to result in a fatal conclusion.

All this occurred in the vicinty of the Cathedral, which, the Irish were told, was in danger of attack from American Protestants. Many of them entrenched themselves in the body of the Cathedral, from whence, during the night, guns were regularly fired at intervals. What purpose this was for, we cannot tell, though it was supposed by several who live thereabout (and from whom we have the account principally) that the firing was intended as evidence of their being possessed of a good supply of munitions of war, and so scare away any attack.

In view of the shameful concessions made to these people, of late, by the Tammany party—and the evidence that they can cut pretty much what capers they like, scathless—who need wonder "that such things are?"

[APRIL 16, 1842]

[NATIVE AMERICANISM REPUDIATED]

> The Aurora has been roaring very loudly and ably, though somewhat savagely, on behalf of the Native Americans, during the past week. The roar is a pleasant one and sounds like an honest one. But the 'rora has a bad habit of calling people names. Oh fie!—*Yesterday's Mercury.*

> We see the danger, let us have the remedy. Let us have a Native American party. Harsh as the word may sound, it is our only safeguard.—*Yesterday's News.*

One of the most ardent wishes of our soul is, to see the American people imbued with a feeling of respect for, and confidence in, *themselves*—a feeling that shall impel them to place their own kind, and their own merits *first*. Entertaining a sentiment of this sort, we cannot look round and behold timid servility to a factious gang of foreigners—or the fostering, in our own republic, of trashy and poisonous European literature—or the bending of knees to the dicta of old world critics, merely because their commands come "by authority" —or the influx among us of vapid English, Scotch, French, and German quacks—without lifting our voice, and, in our way, doing all that we can to denounce and condemn those things.

It becomes our people to have a decent and a proper pride in their government and their country. We possess the most glorious constitution, the most enviable freedom, the happiest and best educated mass of citizens, of any nation that ever existed on the face of the earth. It is well for us to exult in this. Travellers, to be sure, talk about the national vanity of the Americans—but we appeal to any observing man if, in our conduct, we do not show a lamentable want of self complacency, of reliance on our intrinsic worth, and of independence of foreign sway.

Yet with all our antipathy for every thing that may tend to assimilate our country to the kingdoms of Europe, we repudiate such doctrines as have characterised the "Native American" party. We could see no man disfranchised, because he happened to be born three thousand miles off. We go for the largest liberty—the widest extension of the immunities of the people, as well as the blessings of government. Let us receive these foreigners to our shores, and to our good offices. While it is unbecoming for us to fawn upon them and flatter their whims, it is equally unnecessary that we should draw the line of exclusiveness, and say, stand off, I am better than thou.

[APRIL 18, 1842]

"Government
is at best
but a necessary
evil"

Part Three

HOW BEARS THE WIND?

T HE SESSION OF CONGRESS is drawing to its close. Politicians and office holders generally will soon be relieved from the pressure of anxiety which always weighs upon them during each session of the national legislature—anxiety caused by the fickleness of opinion, the constant whirl, and rapid moving of pieces on the political chess board, that for the last ten years has characterised all branches of the American government. Many, too, have been waiting with feverish trepidation, for some developments as to whom the great parties of our republic will bring into the field for the next Presidency. The expectants for that high office have themselves been watching and manoeuvering, and stealthily feeling the popular pulse. No doubt, two thirds of the movements and speeches and expressions of opinion made this winter by the great leaders at the capital, have had express reference to their prospect of the succession.

But, as yet, all is in the womb of the viewless future. Darkness covers the face of the political surface, and chaos moves over the waters. Tongue cannot tell, and the accutest eye cannot discover, who stands the best chance of reaching that "bright reward of ever daring minds,"—the Presidency.

The democratic party are polishing up their arms, and drilling their forces, and making the most of every card that is played. A long and active participation in the method of warfare, has given them great advantages over all opponents. Once defeated, and they take care never to be defeated in the same way again. Their discipline is so complete—their scouts so numerous—their generals and commanders so well fitted for their office—and the memory of their past successes so inspiring—that they are indeed a formidable phalanx. It is asserted—and in all probability there is not much doubt of its truth—that Mr. Van Buren desires to run again. Be it so. Assuredly they could not have a candidate who would carry more of the magic influence of talent, official dignity, and personal popularity. Besides, the advocates of Van Buren say—

> "The king's name is a tower of strength,
> Which they of the adverse faction want."[1]

Let him come then. For our own part, we want to see a glorious race, and devil take the hindermost!

Henry Clay has resigned his seat in the senate. Any one with half an eye, can see what bearing this has. It is the first step toward a nomination at Harrisburg.[2] Clay is a splendid politician. He carries himself so loftily—so goes the whole figure—has such a completeness, entire suaveness, sincereness, in all he does—that we admire him. Clay, however, has little caution. His forte is a bold, dashing kind of warfare. He resembles some fire brained political Murat, riding gallantly into the midst of the enemy, pressing on their very bayonet points, with cuts and thrusts to the right and left, but fearing nothing, and heeding no warning, whether it come from friend or foe. Clay's friends are very enthusiastic, and without doubt they will do their best to put him through.

Then there is the godlike Daniel. As far as we can judge, however, not much likelihood exists of the honorable secretary being entered for the purse at all. 'Tis true, this is a great pity; but most unluckily, it still is true. Webster's example, as far as decorum of social manners is concerned, would be so highly beneficial.

> " 'Tis praiseworthy in this vicious age,
> To see a young man true to his own spouse;
> O, 'tis a vicious age!"

General Scott knocked all his prospects into a disarranged chapeau, by that silly manifesto[3] of his, several months since. We don't think he stands much chance. However, the wheel may turn round, and great things, more than are dreamed of in our philosophy, may yet come to pass.

John C. Calhoun[4] is another expectant. He is a statesman, and, we have no doubt, a patriot. But that nullification business—ah, there's the rub!

Thomas Hart Benton, after all, may be the man that will come up to the post with ribbons flying. Benton is very popular in the south and west. He keeps himself quiet; but in all probability he is doing an active business under the rose.

As for John Tyler, his prospects for re-election are about as safe from demolishment, as a nicely roasted duck at a corporation dinner.

And now it might not be amiss for us to wind up this article with saying who is *our* preference. We shall do no such thing. The influence of the Aurora is no makeweight to be thrown in the scale at a venture. Its advocacy is a stroke of good fortune, which any man,

or any party, may be proud enough and pleased enough to gain.
We shall shape our course by circumstance.[5]

[MARCH 11, 1842]

A PEEP BEHIND THE SCENES

Let no one be surprised when we utter our opinion that the high
functionaries, and chief officers of the American government, just
now, are less distinguished for abilities than any executive or any
cabinet the city of Washington ever held in its limits before. We
imagine there are very few intelligent men who will not agree with
us in this.

The president[6] himself has no strongly marked features. He is a
kind of milk and water politician—one of that class of leaders who
never stir men's minds to strike for them or against them—neither
fish, flesh, or fowl, but possessing some of the traits of each. Such
a being, though often estimable in private life, is the last man on
earth for an important public office.

Webster is, and has always been, much overrated. It is the fashion,
we know, to speak of his gigantic intellect, and his sledge hammer
eloquence; but few who know *the man*, will give him credit for more
than third rate talents. We heard what were considered his best
speeches previously to the election in 1840;[7] and, though biassed in
favor of his oratorical powers, we could see little more than the mere
common place politician. The other secretaries are as characterless
as Tyler himself.

In truth, we are all much under the dominion of humbug in these
matters. We give leading office holders far, far more credit for su-
periority than one in a thousand deserves. For few men know how
the world is governed. The mass look aloft and see the great in their
holiday clothes, prepared to bear the scrutiny of all eyes, and clothed
in dignity as a mantle; and they, the lookers on, are struck with admiration. They think those whose foreheads beam with such majesty,
must be of a higher and holier make than the rest of the world.

But to him who has an opportunity of looking behind the scenes,
all present a different aspect. The glitter, and the glory, and the
majesty, fade away. He sees that people of rank are nothing more
than those of common grade. And he sees, too, all the manoeuvres,
the tricks, the claptrap, and the wire pulling, which the spectators in
front know nothing of. He beholds now the men called great, descend

to mean expedients, and sly artifices, to obtain objects of selfish ambition; how they are marked by frailties, and weaknesses, and follies, and all else that detracts from the perfection of our nature; how they give way to their tempers, and appetites; how, while to the world they present the appearance of being always self possessed, they are, in reality, often at fault, vascillating, and in fever of doubt.

[MARCH 14, 1842]

[THE TRUE DEMOCRATIC PRINCIPLE] [8]

"The best government is that which governs least."

A great and wise moral is interwoven in the above line, which we have taken from the title page of the *Democratic Review*,[9] the leading magazine published this side of the Atlantic. The timid may start, and those bound up in the dominion of the old white headed dotard, Custom, may lift up their hands in alarm—but, still, the true democratic principle, the genuine principle of the American system— teaches that the "best" governing power is that which puts its power in play "least."

We hesitate not to avow ourselves among the foremost of those who desire our experiment of man's capacity for self government, carried to its extreme verge. Every year, we wish to see the doors thrown wider and wider, and the path made broader and broader. We delight in the progress of that doctrine which teaches to elevate the low, and bring down the high.

Fearful men, and proud men, and selfish men (and such people are as numerous in America as elsewhere) will do their best to retard the progress of this principle—but it cannot be fully stopped by any human power. There is a mighty and conquering impulse spread over the land, which forbids that the democratic code shall stand. For we *have* in this country an aristocratic code.

In the matter of banking, for instance, how much better would it be were our legislature to cease meddling with it, and let the country settle the whole subject itself. Every time that congress or a state legislature meddles in matters of finance, they only plunge the interests of the people deeper and deeper into difficulty.

Every winter our law makers go through with their farce of officious intermeddling—and invariably with results of more evil to the country at large than pressed upon us at the commencement of their session.

It needs that the machinery of government be simplified and narrowed—that a small circle be drawn, and that no stretching out thereof be permitted. Our republic is so extensive, and contains such a variety of interests, that the legislature of the federal government is very apt to create clashings, and bickerings, and jealousies. These are seen to increase year after year, and to become more and more dangerous to the stability of union. The only surety—the only real ground—the only certain shield—lies in letting each state manage its own affairs as unto it may seem best. And better still would it be to let the smaller divisions, the local districts, the individual people, retain the rights and prerogatives of the *free man*, in their own respective hands.

[MARCH 16, 1842]

REFORM IT ALTOGETHER

We begin seriously to think of starting a great hue and cry to get up a party which shall go for having legislative and congressional sessions, only once in three or more years. We don't know but we shall make it once in five years.

Few evils are greater in these blessed United States, than the officiousness—of the law-making powers. They meddle with every thing, and derange every thing—from our intercourse with foreign empires, down to the oyster trade. It is wonderful to see how the great mass are gulled in these matters—they have an idea that the learned fathers in legislation can concoct a panacea for all evils. In plain truth, senators and representatives, and assembly men, are no more and no better than other men. Very frequently, they are, in intellectual calibre, several degrees below the average standard. They are not worthy one tenth the respect and reverence that people pay them.

Perhaps not one man in ten who has noticed the course of events for years past, but will agree with us in the idea that if the legislative ninnies were allowed to meet together only once in a great while, we would be much the better off. Half the evils that have afflicted our land of late, would thus be prevented. Amid our great turmoil about reform, it would be no bad idea for our philanthropists to turn their attention thitherwise.

[MARCH 22, 1842]

AMERICANISM

It is a lamentable thing that in this country we have so deplorable a passion for whatever is foreign—whatever is fashionable over the water. Each department of taste and science, and even political economy, (strange as it may seem) is imbued with a principle which leads to copying from the English or other Europeans—in their similar department. And we bend in slavish adoration to that which ushers itself in with the stamp of foreign approbation. We dare not question the infallibility of London and Edinburgh critics. A man comes among us with certificates from royal colleges, and baronet professors, and diplomas of employment as court purveyor in whatever his line may be—and our obedient republicans bow themselves humbly to the mandate.

Why should this be? Have we not people among *us* as worthy and as capable, as these European itinerants? Have we not scholars as learned, and philosophers as wise? If we have *not,* it is from the neglect and ingratitude of their own countrymen—who refuse to give them encouragement, or bestow their well earned meed of praise.

But we *have.* Native Americans are numerous among us, who equal in scientific attainments the best and noblest of the old world. The great bar is, that they have been brought up in our midst; they want the enchantment of distance, and the settling test of foreign applause.

The *Aurora* prides itself on being imbued with an *American* spirit. We look upon emigrants to our republic with friendly and generous eyes; but many things they bring with them might far better be left at home. Brought up to believe in the doctrine of loyalty, and the superstitions of every kind that mark all the countries of Europe, these people find it difficult, when they come to our shores, to throw off the opinions they have worn so long.

Again we say, we have no disposition to look upon foreigners with prejudiced eyes; for we view all the human family with the broad glance of benovelence and love. We say this, not to curry favor with foreigners; that we should disdain. The *Aurora* has shown that it has no fear or flattery for them.

Let the citizens of this great republic be more just to themselves. Let us respect our own capacities, and not hide our lights under bushels.

[MARCH 23, 1842]

CALHOUN

This pride of southern chivalry is a great man—one of the leading spirits of our national legislature. We have always admired, and do admire Calhoun. We admire his spirit, his vigor, his fiery breath, and his brilliant eloquence. We admire his very faults—his devotion to his native south, and his ardent advocacy of her interests beyond all else.[10]

But his *nullification* conduct—there we stop; we can never admire anything which puts in jeopardy the well being of our beloved Union. Were it not for that nullification blot, there is not much doubt but Calhoun would be the chosen candidate of the great democratic party in 1844.

[MARCH 24, 1842]

WHAT'S THE ROW?

Some weeks or two ago, we gave the readers of the *Aurora* as fair and distinct a view of "political prospects," in our country, as sharp eyes and attentive observation could delineate.[11] All judgment, as to who will be the candidate for President in 1844, is, of course, merely a matter of speculation. No human eye has the power of piercing the dark veil of the future, or calculating exactly the chances of each individual's success. A thousand whirls in the wheel of fortune, may bring to pass expressions of opinion, or separations of friendship, or alliances between enemies—the most distant of which it has not entered into the brain of man to conceive.

As remarked by us in the article alluded to, we do not feel a doubt that Mr. Van Buren will be brought in the field. At the worst, he cannot but rally round him all the ancient might of his party—the accustomed friends—the old adherents—the drilled and disciplined "regulars" of the army. Van Buren has always been faithful to his friends—faithful through triumph and doubt, despair and glory, sunshine and tempest, rank and retirement. Perhaps no man ever went into power through the strength of so little personal enthusiasm in his behalf. Few persons have retired from high station, leaving such ardent attachment, and such warm and personal friends behind them.

Van Buren will have a noble antagonist in Henry Clay! For the friends of Henry Clay seem to be determined to wait no longer for a "lucky moment." They have evidently made up their minds to run *him* into the Presidency, or else let the enemy have it their own way. To all appearances, they will make a long pull, a strong pull, and a pull all together.

Yet who can hold the balance, and weigh what is to be? One year ago, who thought that in two months the then newly elected President[12] would be shrouded in his coffin, and laid away in the bosom of the earth, the great mother of men? Who thought that an obscure, milk and water politician, from Virginia,[13] would be swept onward by the wind of accident, to the most glorious place of power the whole world can afford? Who thought it possible that the whig party, having full swing in every branch of the government, would refrain from chartering a national bank.

Still these marvellous things have come to pass. And in that mighty volume wherein are recorded the events and changes of the future years, haply there may be wonders greater, and occurrences more unimagined, than any we have now spoken of.

[MARCH 28, 1842]

THE BENEFIT OF BENOVELENCE

About ten years ago, as every body will remember, Stephen Girard died in Philadelphia, bequeathing two millions of dollars to the founding of a college to educate orphans.

About four years ago, the munificent sum of five hundred thousand dollars was paid to the order of the United States government, by the trustees of a deceased Englishman, to be expended on an institution "for the increase and diffusion of knowledge among men."

What has become of these moneys?

The Girard fund, some how or other, became entrusted to the functionaries of the United States Bank—swindlers whose selfishness and meanness have made them a by word of shame from Maine to Mississippi. These wretched scoundrels, (whom little children should be taught to execrate,) basely made away with the principal part of the funds—as they made way with every thing else entrusted to their despicable hands. Whether Pennsylvania will ever be able, therefore, to build her "Girard College," remains very doubtful.

With regard to the other matter, Congress, we suppose, are too busily engaged in President making, to give it their attention at present. If the Smithsonian moneys are deposited in the bank vaults, as they very probably are—and if they are left there a few months longer, it is pretty certain that the same disposal of them will ensue as has been the case with the Girard legacy.

Have we not a glorious set of fellows to manage affairs in this country?

[MARCH 30, 1842]

THE FOURTH OF APRIL

At most of the whig head quarters, yesterday, throughout the city, the flags were displayed at half mast, in solemnity of the anniversary of the death of President Harrison. It well becomes the whigs to lament his death. No party in this country ever came into power under more favorable auspices; and now they are broken up, divided, and scattered—a tornado or an earthquake could not have done it more effectually. General Harrison undoubtedly favored Henry Clay as his successor, and his administration would have been a Clay administration. He would have signed a charter for a national bank, and gone for a protective tariff. With his majorities in congress, any reasonable measure of his recommendation would have received the legislative sanction, and the difficulties now so varied would have been rare, because his policy was fixed. The name of Harrison was a cynosure, which guided his party to victory; and when "it shot from its sphere," there was no pilot to weather the storm.

In after times, this period of our national history will appear singular indeed. An administration assumed office with an extraordinary majority of the people in its favor. The head of that administration died, and the next constitutional successor assumed his seat, elected precisely on the same grounds—yet, "ere those shoes were cold," his cabinet divided, split up in opinion, and that successor lost the confidence of the majority of his party, and they turned upon him with greater ferocity than his opponents.

John Tyler's administration will be a warning to politicians of the pitfalls that surround the station of the great. For good or for evil, his measures will have a remarkable influence upon the future destinies of the country. The ultra whig party are determined to support Mr. Clay, and the past conduct of John Tyler either kills or makes him. If the whigs do not unite on Henry Clay, the democratic nominee will be elected by as large a majority as General Harrison. *Nous verrons.*[14]

[APRIL 5, 1842]

HEART RENDING

Who can peruse the accounts brought by every arrival from England, without having his tenderest sympathies touched? Destitution is abroad, in her most fearful aspect—starvation is striding over the fairest districts. Americans, who have revelled in the lap of plenty, can have but a faint conception of the horror of the scenes which are every where to be met with in the manufacturing districts of Great Britain. An anti corn law association recently instituted an enquiry into the actual state of the case, and persons were appointed to the sad duty of visiting the regions of distress, and carefully investigating the matter; and the result of their enquiries was appalling.

It is not in one district alone, says an English publication, but in all districts alike, that we hear the wail of suffering and of deep distress. In the course of the enquiries, discoveries of the most soul harrowing kind have been made—such as would scarcely have been credible but for the ocular proof and demonstration. Mothers, newly become such, laid upon pallets of dirty straw or shavings; half naked children lying huddled together in corners of damp cellars, or sitting shivering over the flickering embers of a half cold grate; fathers bowed down by care, and want, and famine—with no work, no food—listening only to the piteous wailing of the wretched creatures around them—such have been the familiar sights encountered by the visitors of the poor during the last few weeks.

It is added, that more than one third of the Skipton Union are at present subsisting on an average of only fifteen pence per head per week!

Think of these things, Americans!—and remember they are the legitimate offspring of that oppressive government. But while you are rendering grateful ascriptions for the blessings you enjoy, forget not to mingle a petition for the relief of those who suffer.

[APRIL 5, 1842]

THE LATEST AND GRANDEST HUMBUG[15]

During the last three or four days, the Home Leaguers have been holding a convention at the Tabernacle in this city. We went up yesterday to see what they were about; we listened to several speeches from their great guns, and then came away.

Sensible men have of late years been flattering themselves that the old, rusty, antiquated doctrine of a Protective Tariff had been given

the go by. It seems that it is not so. A few cliques of selfish manufacturers, joined with a few sap head simpletons, are raising a great
hue and cry to get up the old system with a new name. We hope the
American nation will not allow these hypocrites to deceive them.
The whole pith and essence of their movement is *self*. Under loud
mouthed demonstrations of patriotism, they would push ahead measures for their own interest. They worship the Almighty Dollar—and
to aid themselves therein, they take the name of national prosperity
in vain.

The Home League are in favor of strong measures to protect
American manufacturers. Now, if this movement came from persons
of impartiality, it would not be *quite* so bad—though it is a silly
movement at best. But when we behold the men whose direct pecuni-
ary interest it is to have high duties, banding with one another, and
with a few frail partisans, to push ahead this revamped humbug—
we may well give utterance to our disgust and condemnation.

Let the Home Leaguers look at England; she presents a glorious
picture of the benefits of high duties A government swarming with
bloated parasites, and pompous lordlings—her treasury wrung from
the bloody sweat of her masses, and distilled through the hot cruci-
ble of poverty, with groans and curses, and howlings of torment—
her thousands of greedy human leeches, fattening on legalised extor-
tion and theft—is she not a pretty example for us to imitate?

And the Home Leaguers cloak themselves under the pretext that it
is necessary to put duties on, for purposes of revenue. Granting this
—let the duties be *no more* than enough to raise revenue. And let no
partiality be shown. What right has one man to expect that the fostering care of government may be given to him more than to his
neighbor?

It would be far better, were the national expenses paid by direct
taxation. These roundabout, circumlocutory ways of getting money
always have more or less villainy interwoven in them. They open a
door for favoritism. People do that, indirectly, which, were it done
directly, would be scouted from one end of the land to the other.
Simplicity, straight forwardness, and honesty, are a trio that go
hand in hand, as much in matters of political economy as private
conduct. The Home Leaguers war with the whole of the three.

[APRIL 8, 1842]

OLD LAND MARKS

Today the suffrage party in little Rhode Island hold meetings for the purpose of practically exercising their rights—rights which they claim under the great Bill of American freedom, but which have hitherto been denied them, because inconsistent with the provisions of their royal charter. Although we are not conversant with the minutia, the minor particulars of the Rhode Island difficulty, we perfectly understand the grand features of the matter. It is undoubtedly a question between the supremacy of wrong, and one sided laws, merely because they have been the old custom—and the natural prerogatives of man, given to him at his birth, and which no charter, no legislature, no enactment can rightly take from him. Were we a resident of Rhode Island, we should be a revolutioniser, in the front rank. As it is, the liberal party have our heartiest wishes for their success.

Most men possess, from their earliest dawn of judgment, a great horror of attacking any thing which has received the sanction of a legislature—whether that legislature lived three hundred years ago, or lives now. What is a legislature? A body of *men*, just like those we see about us—no better than, and very likely not near as bright as, people whom we are hourly in business and intercourse with. They are as liable to error, commit as ridiculous blunders of judgment, are swayed by their tempers, or with their selfish passions, or their personal whims—just like the common mass of society. Looking back through the history of the past, what has there been done by way of legislation to make us place much confidence in *law*, as consistent with *justice?*

We are free to confess, for ourself, that we have no reverence for the statute book, any further than it jibes with our notions of truth and justice. Government is at best but a necessary evil; and the less we have of it, the better.

Let no man think, because we see in this country no throne and no titled nobles, we can have no oppression. Human nature is the same, whether in a republic or a despotism; and human nature is so constituted that a desire to raise one's self above his peers, even through infringing on the rights of those peers, *will* actuate individuals and portions of communities.

Who does not love power? And few are they that are willing to forego the pleasant exercise of more of it than their mates can boast of possessing. There has always existed in the United States a faction professing to think that the main body of the people are unfit to govern. In former times, many of them may have been honest in their belief; but the chilliness and narrowness of their doctrine ought

ever to have damned them—and more especially so now, when experience has proved the fallaciousness of their premises.
[APRIL 18, 1842]

[LEGISLATION AND MORALITY][16]

During the last week of the just closed legislative session, at Albany, some sage moralist brought forward a proposition for making
all practices of licentiousness penal, and to be visited by the severest
terrors of the law. Some of the members favored the proposition, and
some opposed it. In the end, it was laid on the shelf.

Were communities so constituted that to prune their errors, the
only thing necessary should be the passage of *laws*, the task of reform would be no task at all. Utopia would come to pass on double
quick time. Sin and folly would take unto themselves wings, and flee
far away—and every thing exist just as the philanthropist might
desire.

Unfortunately, however, it happens that edicts cannot withstand
ill doing—that enactments are unable to supersede nature.

We said, the other day, that government was at best but a necessary evil. The remark came incidentally, yet it might afford the
motto for a new school of political economy; one which should be
more consistent with the age present, and the circumstances and the
popular intelligence that surround us. The old and monstrous, and
miserable creed, that in order to make men good and happy, you
must *govern* them, is in a pretty fair way to be exploded. We are
beginning to feel, not in theory merely, (that has long been the
case,) but in reality, that every being with a rational soul is an *independent man,* and that one is as much a man as another, and that
all sovereign rights reside within himself, and that it is a dangerous
thing to delegate them to legislatures.

As things are, it will admit of considerable discussion, whether
governments (we except none) do not generate nearly as many evils
as benefits. As things *should be*—ninety nine hundredths of legislative prerogatives lopped entirely away—people might enjoy all the
benefits, without the evils.

We are no friends to the fearful caprice of mobs. But the iron arm
of the thousand fingered *law* is as tyrannical—interferes as unjustly,
and oppresses as cruelly, as ever did the sans culottes of Robes-
pierre's day, or the Protestant rabble of the imbecile Lord George

Gordon. The only difference is, that to the former we have been to the manner born, and used to it all the days of our lives—while the latter appears to us with all the startlingness of unaccustomed horror.

Questionless, the kinds of crime which the proposition spoken of in the first paragraph above, seeks to root out, are such as no honorable citizen can countenance. They are a taint and a filth, and a reproach to any man's character. They draw down all that is beautiful and glorious in the soul—and place their victim on a level with the beasts, gross and sensual. Lascivious persons may shelter themselves under the mantle of prevalent usage—but each rightly constituted heart is disgusted with them.

Something far different from a statute, however, is required to annihilate these things. You cannot legislate men into morality.

The more lumbering and numerous become the tomes in a lawyer's library—the longer and stronger grows the list of penalties for crime—the oftener the farce of the people "in legislative assembly convened" is played—just so much more is popular crime fostered, and just so much more is the holy cause of human progress hampered.

[APRIL 20, 1842]

REFORM IN CONGRESS

Within a few years back, public opinion seems to have taken a dislike towards the long session of our national legislature. That this dislike is formed upon reasons of justice, a brief examination will render conclusive. According to the constitution a session of congress constitutes two years, and two session of congress conform to the presidential term of office. The great objection to congressional legislation is its interminable length of session, and the consequent lack of decision upon important matters relating to the public.

The first meeting of congress subsequent to an election for president has no limit except within itself, until the fourth of March two years thereafter. Now the alteration of the constitution is almost impracticable, nor indeed is it of any use, if the PEOPLE will take the whole matter in hand. It is their own fault—we say it fearlessly —it is the PEOPLE'S own fault, that national legislation is so interminable and vexing. How is it to be remedied? is the enquiry. By the simplest method in the world—the ballot box. For many years, both the national and state legislatures of our whole union have been controlled by the immense number of lawyers they have elected to office—men that in a majority of instances (we do not say all) make our legislative halls mere debating rooms to exercise their lungs to the tune of eight dollars a day, who would not earn that sum a week in any court in the union. Now is not this true? We ask any reflective *elector* to view this matter in a correct light, and he, or they, will answer as to its truth. The fact is, in regard to electing members of the House of Representatives, a few leaders pull the wires, and the mass are deluded into support, because their candidates profess to belong to the same party with themselves. And yet who constitute the men they support? Why, a parcel of designing fellows, that look as much to the general interests of the people of the United States, as the followers of the Great Mogul.

They consider that the people placed them in office to blow their own trumpets, and make wonderful speeches for Buncombe. The matter finally resolves itself into this—the voters *must* regulate their own rights—instead of acquiescing in every nomination made by their own party, they should speak for themselves—instead of nominating for members of congress speaking gentlemen, let them nominate and support reflecting ones. Let this course be pursued throughout the Union, and we would see congress adjourn in a proper time. If our city would send to the national legislature two mechanics, one merchant, and one man of moderate fortune, we should be setting an example that would be followed throughout the country. Our city, in its political bearings and influence, has a great control over a large portion of the union; and our position would be regarded accordingly. Let the farmers and agriculturists throughout the land look at these matters in their places, and say what is the use of sending men to congress for the purpose of talking only? We are the representatives of constitutional powers, and we will use our endeavors to make less work and "more cider."

It is easy to look at the subject in a half satirical light; but a moment's reflection will convince every voter, from Maine to Louisiana, that it will be best for them to know the person they nominate for congress. We have too much talk, talk—instead of sending such men to represent you at Washington, send a sensible mechanic, a sensible merchant, a *sensible* painter, a sensible manufacturer, and now and then a sensible lawyer, and the people of this country will find better laws, shorter legislation, and more honesty. Look to it, ye people.

[APRIL 23, 1842]

"In writing, it is occasionally requisite

to have ideas"

Part Four

MR. EMERSON'S LECTURE[1]

T HE TRANSCENDENTALIST had a very full house on Saturday evening. There were a few beautiful maids— but more ugly women, mostly blue stockings; several interesting young men with Byron collars, doctors, and parsons; Grahamites and abolitionists; sage editors, a few of whom were taking notes; and all the other species of literati. Greeley was in ecstasies whenever any thing particularly good was said, which seemed to be once in about five minutes—he would flounce about like a fish out of water, or a tickled girl—look around, to see those behind him and at his side; all of which very plainly told to those both far and near, that he knew a thing or two more about these matters than other men.[2]

This lecture was on the "Poetry of the Times." He said that the first man who called another an ass was a poet. Because the business of the poet is expression—the giving utterance to the emotions and sentiments of the soul; and metaphors. But it would do the lecturer great injustice to attempt anything like a sketch of his ideas. Suffice it to say, the lecture was one of the richest and most beautiful compositions, both for its matter and style, we have ever heard anywhere, at any time.

[MARCH 7, 1842]

[DEATH OF MCDONALD CLARKE] [3]

"Had you seen him,
Your eyes had witnessed twain, and yet but one—
For in his heart he was an innocent child,
And in his make a man. O, brutal earth,
That ever laugh'dst and jeerd'st, and looked in scorn
Upon this angel, bodied in gross flesh."

KIT MARLOWE.

Although it was not our fortune to be acquainted with the Poor
Poet, the eccentric and unfortunate McDonald Clarke, whose death
last Saturday is the subject of considerable comment in our city press
—we feel grieved at the news. He seems to have been a simple, kindly creature—a being whose soul, though marked by little that the
crowd admire, was totally free from any taint of vice, or selfishness,
or evil passion. From his peculiarities, he was exposed to the ridicule
of vulgar men, who seldom go beyond externals; yet Clarke possessed
all the requisites of a great poet.

Whoever has power, in his writing, to draw bold, startling im-
ages, and strange pictures—the power to embody in language, original, and beautiful, and quaint ideas—is a true son of song. Clarke
was such an one; not polished, perhaps, but yet one in whose facul-
ties that all important vital spirit of poetry burnt with a fierce brightness. From his being so out of the common channel; from his abrupt-
ness, and, if we may so call it, jaggedness, of style—many persons
have not taken the trouble to read the fugitive effusions which he,
through our paper and others, gave to the world. But they are mostly
all imbued with the spiritual flame. We always, on perusing Clarke's
pieces, felt, in the chambers of the mind within us, a moving and
responding, as of harp cords, struck by the wind.

He was very poor. Not of the earth, earthy—not engaged in the
withering toils of traffic—not a votary at the altar of any golden idol
—was he to whose memory we devote this passing tribute. It is a
dreary thought—the likelihood that, through the chillness of destitution, this man, his soul swelling with gorgeous and gentle things,
was prevented the chance of becoming an ornament to the world, instead of its scoff and laughing stock. It is a dreary thought, too, that
poor Clarke's case has its copies so many times repeated among us.
What a devil art thou, Poverty! How many high desires—how many
aspirations after goodness and truth—how many noble thoughts,
loving wishes toward our fellows, beautiful imaginings—thou hast
crushed under thy heel, without remorse or pause! What majestic
beauty thou has condemned to pine unnoticed in the shade—while
sister beauty, with wealth, made drunk the eyes of men! What swelling of hearts thou hast sent down to the Silent House, after a life of
bitterness and strife! What talent, noble as that of famous poets and
philosophers—what minds, fit to govern empires, or instruct the
world—what souls, glowing in secret with the halo of science—thou
dost doom, year after year, to pine in obscurity, or die in despair!

It is well. Clarke was little fitted for elbowing his way amid the
mass; let no one grieve that he has passed away. Let us hope that he
is in that place which we are fond of believing to be peopled by joy
never ceasing, and by resplendent innocence and beauty. On earth,

his love, from its oddness and inconsistence with fashion, was laughed to scorn; up above, it will find itself amid kindred elements.

We understand that papers are up at several places, to receive subscriptions for erecting a monument to the memory of the hapless poet. We commend the subject as a deserving one. And, strangely enough, several years ago, a scheme was jocosely suggested of an exactly similar purport. Clarke heard of it, and wrote the following which we are permitted to publish. It is singular that this effusion, which was written June 11, 1835, should come in play as it now does:—

THE DEAD POET

'Tis but barren respect they are paying him now!
    It can flatter but selfish passions, only—
When the laurel first blooms on his mouldering brow,
    Genius must mourn that its fate is so lonely.

Human pomp is a pitiful thing—
    But to decorate death is indeed disgusting!
Let the green sprig rise, and the red herb spring
    Where no slab in the wind and rain is rusting!

He was left by these sunrise friends, to droop,
    When his doom would have turned on the roll of a dollar!
For a spirit like his, that scorned to stoop,
    Could never a selfish interest follow.

But his form must rise, like the sun, in his might,
    Blast Envy's fog by its own strong lustre,
Or in silence go down with a clouded light,
    Till memory's stars o'er its ashes cluster.

Oh, let him rest in his nameless place—
    The few who knew and loved him, know it—
They will guard it from Ostentation's face,
    That would shame, not soothe, the sainted Poet.

Majestic marks of crumbling stone,
    Are for those whose memory else would perish;
But the human heart is the urn alone.
    A poet's pride would wish to cherish!

We hope, however, that no reader will be discouraged from contributing his moiety to the memorial proposed, because of the above sentiments of Clarke. They only prove the more fully his deservedness of the poetic wreath.

We have strung out our notice far beyond what we originally intended for its dimensions. Perhaps, however, the space thus used may not be unprofitably used. It may teach that genius, after all, is a dangerous trait. Its fires, to be sure, sometimes enlighten and beautify, but quite often scorch, wither, and blast the soul of its possessor. Like Phæton's privilege, the mighty gift conferred, may bring death and ruin.

Peace to thy memory, Afara! In

> "the sphere which keeps
> The disembodied spirits of the dead,"

may the love of angels, and the ravishing splendor of the Country Beautiful, and the communion of gentle spirits, and sweet draughts from the Fountain of all Poetry, blot out every scar of what thou hast suffered here below!

[MARCH 8, 1842]

[HAPLESS AFARA!]

> "The artillery of that mind was hot
> As the thunderbolts of thought;
> But his name won't be forgot
> Tho' he died not as he ought.
> Damned—deserted—love—love sick.
>
> From his ashes, even the storm,
> Of the Christmas night he fell,
> Was his skeleton dragged—
> All warm—
> Though his brain was black with the storms o' hell."

MCDONALD CLARKE

We have come across the above effusion of the poor poet whose death was noted the earlier part of the week. The verses, (so characteristic of their author's style,) though inscribed on the margin "For the Aurora," have never before been published; the paper on which it is written is itself a mere tatter, burnt and crumpled—a fit emblem of the mind of him who traced the lines upon it!

Let no one be surprised when we say that we love to dwell upon the theme of this poor fellow's death. It is well for men to turn aside once in a while from the noise and din of the great Babel—from the scarring cares, and the gross anxieties of the other world—and give way to the reflections which such an event as Clarke's decease very naturally awakens. These reflections cannot but have a gentle influence; they cannot but shine down upon the heart, like the sunlight upon a flower bud, starting and swelling the blossom into fragrant and full blown life.

On one end of the scrap of paper containing the verses we have given above, the following is written:

"Poor Clarke dashed his brains out against the Emmet monument."

Then over on the other side:

> "Poor fellow! he is gone.
> How wild last night. How calm
> May the coming Christmas morn
> Find————"

The words seem prophetic. The "coming Christmas morn," will indeed find him calm—a calmness which his life knew nothing of.

On the back of the torn scrap before us is written (in Clarke's own hand, as is all that we have given above) the following, headed "Lines on the death of McDonald Clarke."

> "From the *Angel of Charity*."
>
> "Men will trample on his grave,
>   And keep the grass from growing there;
> And not e'en one poor flower will wave
>   Above him in the summer air."
>
> *Fitz Green Halleck.*
>
> "O say not so!
> Whatever earth may think—
>   *   *   *"

We have heard that much blame is bestowed on the foolish person who deceived Clarke by promising to introduce him to the lady whose beauty had maddened him. It is just. The being who could trifle with the blasted brain, or the eccentric operations of a love, pure and fiery, though uncouth—deserves to be received among men with frowns and with the curled lip of scorn.

Hapless Afara! He sleeps now where the jeer and the scoff shall touch him no more—where the vulgar world may not reach him with its ridicule or its cares. The grave of his rest is one of the earth's pleasant places—such a grave as himself would have chosen. In that quiet and dreamy spot, it is fitting for him to repose—him whose passage through the world has not been "safe from the storms of time," but wild, fretful, and full of tumult.

[MARCH 12, 1842]

PARK THEATRE[4]

The play of the Tempest was revived last night, in a very respectable manner; but it did not go off so well as we could have wished. The house was not bad, nor was it what might have been expected—and the players seemed to be out of sorts with their several parts. Barry played with his cutomary grace and dignity, and Miss Buloid and Susan Cushman were both very interesting as the fair daughters of Prospero. Mrs. Pritchard, as our friend of the Mercury would say, displayed a pair of pretty legs "with much archness" while walking about, and with infinite grace when lying flat on the stage, and shamming dead.

Mrs. Knight was not quite the Ariel of our youthful dreams, but for lack of a better, she did very well. Placide, Fisher, and Billy Williams tried to be very funny—monstrously so, and we began to think they had succeeded, as the finale drew nigh. Indeed, with respect to Steppano, we should say that nothing which he did, while in the part, became him like the gusto he displayed when bearing it. Caliban was a rare monster, and his incantations were of the most unnatural order. Indeed Billy surpassed himself, and we hope the play will be repeated.[5]

[MARCH 22, 1842]

BAMBOOZLE AND BENJAMIN[6]

We have in America many literary quacks. Persons possessing some little tact at stringing together sentences, and very great tact of impudence, conceit, and brazen assumption, now and then rise up among us, and push their fancied merits into notoriety. If they are lucky enough to get into the chair editorial, thereby obtaining a chance to puff themselves directly and indirectly, they straightway give themselves great airs, and imagine they are very important characters in the drama of life.

Of the kind described, is the great Ann Street[7] Bamboozle, Park Benjamin, editor of the New World newspaper. He is one of the most vain pragmatical nincompoops in creation—sets himself up for a poet! and has lately perpetrated a mass of trash which he calls a comedy![8]

In the paper he conducts, he professes much regard for religion and piety, while those who know him well, are perfectly aware that

he is as rank an infidel as ever sat under the ministrations of Kneeland[9] or followed in the train of Fanny Wright.[10] He is not a native
of the United States, but came here a foreigner.[11]

Some time ago, this Benjamin opened himself as a kind of author's
intelligence office—advertising his services to procure a market for
those literary men who wished that trouble taken off their hands.
We are pretty authentically informed that several scribblers who were
silly enough to place confidence in his *honesty,* found themselves
fleeced with a vengeance.

We should hardly take the trouble to show up this enormous bab-
oon, were it not that people abroad may be led to think him a sample
of our American authors. In New York, we all understand his merits.
He is looked upon as well bred men, in company, look upon a pert,
ungainly fellow, half boor and half fop—who has, by some mistake,
gained admittance into the society of decent and fashionable people.
He has no caste among the refined and accomplished circles of our
city.

Occasionally this Benjamin undertakes to criticise. If the reader
can imagine how a blacksmith with a half tempered piece of scythe
blade would perform a delicate surgical operation—he can then imagine something about the critical abilities of this witless ape.

We beseech those of our readers who have hitherto, by sufferance,
given in to the self pressed claims of the great Bamboozle—that they
will not be thus credulous any longer. The utmost stretch of his *talents* is the concocting of what he calls "sonnets," whose length,
though merciully confined to the allotted fourteen line limits, is pro-
verbially great in the way of sleeping draught. He has lately degraded
the very name of literature by a series of clap traps and low vulgar
tricks to advance the interests of his paper—which ought to make
him scouted by every periodical in the land. We should touch further
upon this point, but are assured that full and severe justice will
shortly be done it by a contemporary, who entertains the same
notions upon the matter as ourselves.

Benjamin is inseparably interwoven with Bamboozle "any how."

[MARCH 24, 1842]

THE PENNY PRESS[12]

Among newspapers, the penny press is the same as common
schools among seminaries of education. They carry light and knowl-

edge in among those who most need it. They disperse the clouds of ignorance; and make the great body of the people intelligent, capable, and worthy of performing the duties of republican freemen. The senseless prattle that those having mighty ideas of their own importance, now and then indulge in towards these mighty engines of truth, is as disgraceful to the utterers themselves, as it is false in principle. The large papers *feel* that we are supplanting them. They *know* that the time must soon arrive, when they will have to hang up their harp upon the willows, and lay themselves down and die quietly, and be laid in their graves. No exertions of theirs can postpone this doom. It *must* come.

Nor is it only the lower and middling classes who take the cheap papers. They are found in the houses of the rich. They lie upon magnificent centre tables, and are met with in the parlors of the wealthy and proud. Every where is their influence felt. No man can measure it, for it is immeasurable.

Almost the only sensible move Tyler has made since his induction into the Presidency, is the currying of favor with the penny press.[13]

[MARCH 26, 1842]

THE NEW YORK PRESS

It is almost impossible to calculate the number of papers that are printed in the city of New York.[14] We shall only attempt, therefore, to give a short sketch of the leading ones.

Without vanity, we can say that the *AURORA* is by far the best newspaper in the town. It is bound to no party, but fearless, open, and frank in its tone—brilliant and sound, pointed without laboring after effect, ardent without fanaticism, humorous without coarseness, intellectual without affectation—and altogether presents the most entertaining melange of latest news, miscellaneous literature, fashionable intelligence, hits at the times, pictures of life as it is, and everything else that can please and instruct—far beyond any publication in the United States. Its chief editor, and his coadjutors, are among the ablest writers of America; and each one "knows his part, and does it well."

Perhaps the next best paper as regards abstract merit, is the *EVENING POST*.[15] This daily is unexceptional, what there is of it; but the reputation of a refined poet, and the course that must be pursued in order to make a readable paper, clash with each other.

To our mind, and we have not hesitated ever to express the opinion, Bryant is the best poet who writes in the English language. His fame will endure as long as Americans retain a love for the beauty of sentiment or delicacy of style From what we now say, however, let no one infer that we think the Post what a newspaper ought to be; our opinion is very different from that.

The *COMMERCIAL ADVERTISER*[16] stands next upon the list. Col. Stone is a good writer, and never perpetrates any thing but what is good, as far as its style is concerned. The Commercial is generally a candid paper, and never keeps back its sentiments from fear. To our minds this is a merit which covers a multitude of sins. We commend the Commercial.

The *AMERICAN*[17] is somewhat of the same order as the Commercial, but not near equal to it in ability, and also far beneath it in sincerity. No man who reads the American can fail to form an opinion that its editor is a man of violent prejudices, and somewhat narrow ideas.

Religious people who wish a sixpenny daily, take the *JOURNAL OF COMMERCE*.[18] The Journal generally has late news; but no doubt its editors are hypocritical, and have very few of the sentiments they profess.

The *EXPRESS*[19] is rather a stupid affair in some respects, though, if it had not come out lately with a ridiculous attack upon the small papers, we should be inclined to speak favorably of it in others.

The *COURIER and ENQUIRER*[20] is a violent and vindictive partisan print, professing to be an organ of whiggery. Some of the whigs acknowledge it, and some do not.

The *TRIBUNE*[21] is a tolerable paper, conducted with much fairness, and ability, and perhaps receives about as much of the confidence of its party as any press in the United States.

Our near neighbor, the *SUN*,[22] is known to every body; for not to know the Sun argues one's self unknown. Though the Sun is conducted with no great spirit, it has its merits; and we venture to say obtains as large a circulation as any paper on the continent, or perhaps in the world.

The *STANDARD*[23] is a rickety affair, which nobody ever sees. Such a paper might have satisfied people twenty years ago, but at the present age it is as much out of date as cocked hats, or trains to ladies' gowns.

The *HERALD*[24] is a paper which nothing that we can say can convey our opinions more strongly of. It is a scandal to the republic.

The *NEW ERA*[25] has a circulation somewhere between 800 and 1000. It is dying very fast, and is only sustained by corporation favor.

Very few really good papers are published in New York. Most of
them are bound up in partisanship, or prejudice, and are incapable
of taking enlarged and comprehensive views of matters and things.
Five sixths of them are directly or indirectly under the control of
foreigners; they therefore, though possessing some marks of ability,
are not imbued with any wholesome American spirit. They *cannot*
and *do not* come out with that fiery enthusiasm in the cause of truth
and liberty—that vigor of advocacy—that energy and boldness and
frankness which will ever mark the apostle of the new system—the
system which teaches far different doctrine from the rusty, cankered,
time-honored, anti-democratic philosophy that looms up in Europe,
and is planting its poisonous seeds too widely among us.

[MARCH 29, 1842]

DICKENS AND DEMOCRACY[26]

We yesterday received the April number of the *Democratic Review*. It contains good reading—rather more than its usual proportion of solid and political articles. The leader is headed "The
Reception of Mr. Dickens." We read it with pleasure through three
or four pages, when, all of a sudden, how were our eyes startled by
seeing the critic join issue with Boz, and attack that writer with a
fierceness and openness that might almost be worthy of "the regular
army."

The *Review* says, speaking of Dickens and his novels:

> "There is one striking defect in them, which, in the present
> undiscriminating applause bestowed on both him and them, we
> will not omit to notice. We allude to the atrocious exaggeration of
> his bad characters. There are no such creatures in the world, or in
> nature. Take Quilp, that hideous and devilish incarnation of the
> pure abstract of all that is malignant;—what right has Boz to dis-
> gust and wound all our moral sensibilities, by giving such a thing
> a prominent place?"

Then again:

> "True, we cannot close our doors against either him or them,
> if we would, *** still, there are no such characters in human
> nature; and the moral effect of exhibiting such to the imagination
> is very bad; and a serious drawback on the useful influence of
> the rest of his writings. *** The same tone of exaggeration runs
> indeed through most of his characters."

Lest we should be accused of not treating the critic fairly, we will add, that the general tone of the article in question is highly favorable to Mr. Dickens, and that it expresses the utmost satisfaction with the complimentary course pursued by the Americans toward their great literary guest. We shall now use liberty to make a few remarks about the exceptions taken by the writer in the *Review*.

Boz appears to be no Utopian. Though such books as his could have been written only by a man whose heart had great store of kindly feelings, confidence in the capability of his fellow men for the attainment of high perfection, genial dispositions—and possessed, also, of a propensity to look on the bright side of life's picture; yet Boz, like the rest of us, knows, no doubt, that there are many wicked men in the world—many beings whose hearts are fearful pest houses, and whose presence is as the taint of some deadly contagion. And it is necessary to exhibit these creatures in their unclothed deformity. Many well meaning, but weak minded people, have an unwholesome delicacy upon this subject. Hold up villainy to public scorn, say we; the wise physician cures no cankers except by cutting with a sharp blade, and a deep stroke.

Is the *Review sure* that "no such characters exist in the world or in nature," as Dickens' villains? Would to heaven that it could reasonably be sure! Why, almost within the reach of our voice, there is the palpable counterpart to the worst embodiment of evil that the brain of Dickens ever transcribed upon paper! And the being to whom we allude is *worse* than the wickedest character in the Boz novels—inasmuch that the poison he diffuses is gilded, and allowed to pass by common sufferance. A reptile marking his path with slime wherever he goes, and breathing mildew at everything fresh and fragrant; a midnight ghoul, preying on rottenness and repulsive filth; a creature, hated by his nearest intimates, and bearing the consciousness thereof upon his distorted features, and upon his despicable soul; one whom good men avoid as a blot to his nature—whom all despise, and whom no one blesses—*all this* is James Gordon Bennett. Joined to the craftiness and utterly selfish beastliness of Fagan—the infernal depravity, the gloating, satanic delight in torturing, of Quilp —the dull, callous insensibility to any virtue, of Sikes—this loathsome agent of damnation claims the additional merit of having been spawned, not in an American gutter, but to have ornamented with the presence of his earlier age, some sty, pauper out house, or reeking bagnio, of his native North Britain![27]

The *Democratic Review* need not go far, then, to find its own arguments overthrown. In truth, the editor of the *Review* misses the consistency of his own doctrines. It is characteristic, indeed, of a noble mind to look around upon fellow creatures with broad glances of comprehensive love, and generous confidence in their essential capacity for virtue. Yet of him whose opportunity it may be, stern duty requires that he should sometimes paint lofty vice—that he should picture it forth in all its glaring reality—and that he should thus teach how terrible a thing is iniquity, and how wise it is to avoid the paths of evil.

[APRIL 2, 1842]

A WORD TO CORRESPONDENTS

We wish that those who favor us with accounts of balls, or any other public "doings," would make it an imperative rule to exclude any thing in the shape of ill nature, or that may have the appearance of vindictiveness. We are always pleased at the attention of those who kindly furnish these effusions; but we are never willing to wound any body's feelings, or touch sorely upon the little peculiarities of private people. Amid the multiplicity of our duties, we, of course, cannot carefully revise the MSS. of correspondents; of course, therefore, many things creep in that we would gladly exclude.

[APRIL 6, 1842]

WE

During the past week, the *Aurora* has met with almost unprecedented success. Our regular edition has been completely exhausted by eight or nine o'clock every morning; and we have made arrangements to increase it next week to a thousand beyond what it has hitherto been.[28]

It is almost needless to add that our mind swells with gratitude to those inhabitants of our city, and elsewhere, who thus kindly evince that they like us and appreciate us. Editing a daily paper, to be sure, is an arduous employment. The consciousness that several thousand people will look for their *Aurora* as regularly as for their breakfasts, and that they expect to find in it an intellectual repast—something *piquant,* and something solid, and something sentimental, and something humorous—and all dished up in "our own peculiar way"—

this consciousness, we say, implies no small responsibility upon a man. Yet it is delightful. Heavy as it weighs, we have no indisposition to "take the responsibility."

Every day that passes over our heads, encourages us more and more in our determination to render Aurora *the* paper of the city. Though we do not expect to set the North river on fire, we are free to confess, without vanity, that we have full confidence in our capacities to make Aurora the most readable journal in the republic. We are hourly accosted in the streets, in hotels, in places of mercantile resort, every where, with compliments, and praises of the boldness, beauty, and merit of our paper. And for the last fortnight hardly a day has arrived at its sundown without showing upon our subscription books a score or so more patrons than we had in the morning.

Again, from our inmost hearts, we thank our countrymen. Our *countrymen!* the phrase rolls pleasantly from our tongue. We glory in being *true Americans*. And we profess to impress Aurora with the same spirit. We have taken high American ground—not the ground of exclusiveness, of partiality, of bigotted bias against those whose birth place is three thousand miles from our own—but based upon a desire to possess the republic of a proper respect for itself and its citizens, and of what is due to its own capacities, and its own dignity. There are a thousand dangerous influences operating among us—influences whose tendency is to assimilate this land in thought, in social customs, and, to a degree, in government, with the moth eaten systems of the old world. Aurora is imbued with a deadly hatred to all these influences; she wages open, heavy, and incessant war against them.

We can assure our friends who, hereabouts and at distant places, have kindly expressed their satisfaction at the course we have taken, that our paper will continue to be characterized by the same qualities of impartiality, fearlessness, and an unflinching determination to lay on the lash wherever it is deserved.

And so, with prospects cloudless and aspirations lofty, and evidences of public favor which, we proudly boast, were never vouchsafed so extensively to any young newspaper in the land, we bid our readers God's benison! and next Monday, with beams new furbished, we shall be on hand like our old Olympian namesake, of the time of the Trojan wars, who,

> "Fair daughter of the dawn,
> Sprinkled with rosy light the dewy lawn."29

[APRIL 9, 1842]

ITALIAN OPERA IN NEW ORLEANS

> We perceive by the New Orleans papers that "Sonnambula" has been brought out there, and that Mrs. Sutton has produced quite a sensation in the principal character. The "corps" has been playing for some time in that capital—but hitherto, from some underhand intrigue, Mrs. Sutton was kept in the background.— *Morning Herald.*

The above piece of stupid humbug is, of course, from Bennett's pen. No other paper in the country but his ever attempted to soft soap La Signora Fatoni Sutton—as she desired him to style her— into a *prima donna.* Only read the puff direct, and the stupidity is obvious. First he says she has made quite a sensation, and, secondly, that by some underhand intrigue, she was kept in the back ground. Was there ever such inconsistency? The fact is, La Signora *Fat*-oni is only a second rate singer, and about a third rate musician. She had a fair chance at the Park, in Norma,[30] and could not succeed in drawing even the expenses. As a concert singer, she was thrown into the shade by Borghese,[31] and yet she had the temerity to go to Havana and New Orleans to test the public favor with that accomplished artist.

We hope they will keep La Signora Fatoni at the south, for here we have some real musical and dramatic talent which is quite unavailable. At the present time we have Mr. and Mrs. Seguin,[32] and Manvers, wanting an engagement at the Park. We have Miss Ayres and Miss Horn, with Chapman, Lambert, Tom Placide, John Sefton, T. D. Rice, and several others. Next week we shall have Forrest and Clifton here, so that we do hope our fair, fat, and forty friend, La Signora, as she loves to be called, will stay away until we send for her, and that will be a long while first. Nobody but Bennett ever tried to persuade the people that Mrs. Sutton could sing—but heaven spare us from ever seeing her attempt to act again!

[APRIL 15, 1842]

NEWSPAPERIAL ETIQUETTE

It is customary, our readers no doubt are well aware, for the six-penny dailies to plume themselves on their "influence." They assume a position of pompous dignity, and affect a very soverign contempt for their little popular contemporaries. In editorial intercourse, the sixpennies seldom deign to notice the pennies, and two pennies—after the fashion of that code of politeness, prevalent in certain circles, which teaches to "cut" any man who is not, as the Hon. Mrs. Bolton Comfort says, "one of *us*."

We have frequently been amused at specimens of this kind of behavior. Men of sense, certainly, are not in the habit of gauging the deserts of what they read in a periodical, either by the size of that periodical, or by its being bought for a cent. It would be as reasonable to suppose in walking through Broadway, that every exquisitely dressed person you meet is a gentleman or a millionaire, and *vice versa.*

Had we in America a monarchial or an aristocratical form of government, it is very probable that the sixpenny papers might exercise a greater sway than the small ones. As things are, however, the converse of this supposition is really the case. Here, the mass of men comprise the governing power, "the people." And while the cheap papers have influence with this mass, they can well afford to let their inflated neighbors parade their (somewhat laughable) claims to exclusiveness and the top of the ladder.

[APRIL 18, 1842]

[HOW TO WRITE A LEADER]

Yesterday was dull, stupid, misty, cold, wet, and disagreeable in every respect. We dawdled through the earlier hours, those between breakfast and dinner time—and at the period of present writing can call to mind no occurrence worthy being noted down in this article, (which we intend, before we get through to make very interesting and very amusing).

That was an observant French writer who, perpetrating a novel, commenced it somewhat thus wise.—In one of the horrible months when fogs and damps fill the atmosphere, and Englishmen, by dozens, commit *suicide.* We say he was an observant and a wise fellow who wrote this; for gentle reader, whether you have ever observed it or not, there is an intimate connection between lowering weather and love of laudanum—between heavy air and hysterics, (sagacious corollaries, those, ain't they?)

Such a day as yesterday, for instance, who, if ever so easily satisfied, *could* be in love with life? Mud and slops made every thoroughfare impassable; and a strange, mysterious kind of stagnating influence spread far and near, in doors as well as out. What man with nerves and obtusities strong enough to defy that influence? Assuredly not hapless we—we are but mortal flesh and blood.

Then there came a voice, like that which, eld, struck the ear of the apostolic John—saying, write.

The New York Aurora is a periodical issued every morning, from Nassau street, near Tammany Hall. It professes to give news, with the various phases of life, and all the etceteras that are needful to appertain. Most of the principal articles are concocted by one Whitman, whilom little known in these diggings; which latter part of the category is daily becoming more and more oblivious. It requires no great stretch of ingenuity to suppose that in order to keep some eight or ten compositors employed, a man's pen might fly glibly, and still be by no means too much in a hurry. Something or other *must* be "set up."

Having thus explained, (it is always best to begin at the beginning, and make a clear sweep,) the field is now fair before us.

In the arrangements for the New York Aurora, an uncontrollable law exists, (immutable, like the edicts of the Medes and Persians, which alter not,) that every paper should have a *leader*. A leader is always expected to be something particularly well written, and particularly worth reading. We hope we have now made the whole matter sufficiently lucid.

In writing, it is occasionally requisite to have *ideas*. The reader will note that we say *occasionally* necessary; we might subject our veracity to malignant aspersions, did we not distinctly make this semi reservation. Furthermore, that there *can* be very fine writing, without ideas, the history of literature affords many brilliant examples. It might seem a piece of vanity for us to arrest the attention of the lady or gentleman who does us the honor of perusing our Aurora, *here*.

We commenced this essay by some remark upon the state of the weather, during the twenty-four hours previous to twelve o'clock, midnight, last. To speak of weather argues, perhaps, no great loftiness of ideas, of aspiration of intellect. Observations upon that subject, indeed, are rather common, than otherwise. For illustration—Suppose Higgins meets Snuggs:

"Wet day," says Higgins.

"Bad for coughs," rejoins Snuggs.

"Very bad," answers Higgins, looking abstractedly up aloft at the murkiness.

"Fine weather last Saturday," continues Higgins, by way of suggesting something very new and bright.

"Great change from this," replies Snuggs, determined not to let his companion go ahead in originality.

"So it is," says Higgins, as if the fact had never struck him half so forcibly before.

"Dark days are not as fine as sunshiny ones," answers Higgins.

Apparently, the other considers this remark incontrovertible; for he looks up at the clouds again, and utters not a word.

"Wind will change tomorrow," asserts Higgins.

Here is a chance, where, as the politicians, men may honestly differ in opinion.

"Don't think so," replies Snuggs.

"Certainly will," reasserts Higgins.

"Altogether impossible," re-replies Snuggs.

&c., &c., &c.

We presume the reader, as his or her eye glances over the dialogue, will conclude it, without demur, to be a "sketch from real life."

Undoubtedly, no person can now have any reason for doubting that the weather is, by custom, a legitimate theme for persons to exercise their voices (and pens) upon.

The thing is done—the *leader* is prepared! *Laus Deo!*

[APRIL 19, 1842]

J. F. COOPER

This great gawky has been making a still greater ass of himself, if possible, lately, by procuring at the hands of juries certain small potato verdicts, against a poor devil of an editor, a poor devil of an author, and God only knows how many more poor devils beside.[33] For our own part, we don't see how any twelve men of sense could be led to pronounce in favor of this enormous ape.

The grounds for founding a libel prosecution on are so flimsy, so utterly destitute of any reason, that who can but be filled with amaze at the result? Cooper is damning himself utterly in the estimation of all sensible men.

[APRIL 19, 1842]

HORACE GREELEY

It is well known among politicians, that the personage whose name heads this article is a perfect walking budget of facts, tables, and statistics. He knows all about imports and exports, banks, finances, elections, party prospects, and every thing else that can be learned by careful investigation of registers, directories, and political almanacs.

Yet, as if to illustrate the inconsistency of philosophy with figures, we question whether a man in the empire state entertains so many absurd tenets in religion, such fallacious opinions of government and political economy, such short sighted notions of what are the land's true interests—as this same Mr. Horace Greeley.

The Tribune promulgates abolitionism, Fourierism, socialism, universalism, national bankism, high tarriffism, and half a dozen other similarly contradictory systems. It might be amusing in no small degree, to hear Mr. G. attempt to reconcile these doctrines with one another. Hardly any two of them can go together with any more safety than the fox, goose, and corn, in the old nursery tale.

[APRIL 19, 1842]

"We determined

to perpetrate

a few paragraphs

of sentiment."

Part Five

ABOUT SILENCE

S ILENCE? WHAT CAN NEW YORK—noisy, roaring, rumbling, tumbling bustling, stormy, turbulent New York —have to do with *silence?* Amid the universal clatter, the incessant din of business, the all swallowing vortex of the great money whirlpool, the strife and the warfare, and the fever and the trembling—who has any, even distant, idea, of the profound repose, the hushed lethargy of silence?

It may be thought by some sagacious reader of this article, that writing about silence is equivalent to writing about nothing at all —in the same way that black is considered the absence of all color. To our mind, however, it is a very prolific subject. There are people who can descant much more largely upon *nothing* than upon *something;* though we desire not to be classed among the number, we opine that much may be said upon the theme which we have chosen for these present cogitations.

A quiet repose is a peculiarity of high breeding, and gentlemanly or ladylike taste. In the most refined circles of society, you cannot but note this; you cannot but observe what a perfect absence of bustle there is; what a simplicity—a kind of antifussiness—a stillness without being awkward—an absence of uncouth animation, that yet is far from assimilating to prosiness. A general characteristic of being perfectly at home and perfectly easy, requiring no straining, no effort, to show you that you are not abashed, runs through like a tint of color, and gives that charming, indescribable hue which pervades the best classes, either in our glorious New York, or in any other city. Loud and boisterous talking in polite company is looked upon as extremely vulgar; you can be vivacious, lively, facetious, if you will; but let all be done quietly and smoothly. So will it come with double zest.

Fashion is a capricious jade! She cannot exist unless in the very focus of all motion and bustle—and yet she retreats to an inner sanctum—a kind of sacred circle, which no one must cross—and there votes it decidedly clownish to make any departure from a perfect abandonment to quiet.

One of earth's pleasantest places, (positively we are growing sentimental,) is an old shady country village, of a warm summer afternoon. All is hushed and sleepy. The bee's hum, and now and then
the long drawn out piping of a locust, or an occasional note from a
bird—these alone break in upon the profound stillness. And it is
delicious for a lazy man to give way to such influences on such an
occasion, and fall into a kind of drowse—an Elysium of dreaminess
enough to bring in all the charms of imagination—and reality
enough to make the whole affair double flavored.

In our great metropolis, the only time that spirits of silence can
properly call their own, is from about half past two until half past
three o'clock in the morning. The whole city is then asleep. Hardly
any jarring interruption disturbs the darkness like that of death.

[MARCH 19, 1842]

"BLACK AND WHITE SLAVES"[1]

We received, yesterday afternoon, from A. Donnelly, 19½ Courtlandt Street, a lithographed picture inscribed with the words which
head this paragraph. The print represents two different localities—
the one to the right, a scene in England—that to the left, another in
America. The figures of the first, are a laborer's family, his wife lying
dead upon a heap of straw, an infant endeavoring to draw moisture
from her breast, two or three famished children near by, and the
laborer himself seated disconsolately upon a stool by the side of the
corpse. Looking on, is a fat, pompous, lordly parish officer, evidently
no stranger to the good things of life. He is speaking: "Come, pack
off to the work house; that's the only fit place for you!"

The set off to this, is a delineation of domestic life at the south.
A gentleman and lady, with two children, come to pay a call at the
shanty of a family of their slaves. Every thing bears the impress of
cheerfulness and content.

There is a good moral conveyed in this picture. It would be well
if the English abolitionists were to reflect upon it. John Bull raises a
great bluster and outcry, because of the oppressed conditions of the
American negroes. He gets quite sentimental in his sorrow—blub-
bers, and even sometimes goes so far as to contribute moneys for
the support of itinerant abolitionist lectures. And all the while, the
British have within the borders of their own country, miseries com-
pared to which those of the southern slaves are as a ward to Ossa.

In England, nine-tenths of the population do not enjoy the common comforts of life. Their inequality of laws, their oppressive taxation, their established church, and their undue proportion of inhabitants, contribute to bring about this horrible state of things; and they are the people who can come to us with monitorial teachings of what is our duty to "our colored brethren!"

Let our transatlantic neighbors take the beam out of their own eyes—and then they can reasonably find fault with the mote in ours. Let them cease to coin the sweat, and labor, and blood, and misery of the mass, into an inflated prosperity for the few. Let them pull down the lumbering fabric of monarchy and aristocracy that has stood long enough, and too long. Let them destroy the prevalence of the spectacles of famine, penury and death, that make Britain but one vast poor house—and then they can send us some of their charity and their sympathy.

[APRIL 2, 1842]

OVER THE OCEAN

The calm which prevails in the civilised world at the present time is of thrilling moment. It resembles the stillness which mariners, who sail in tropical seas, tell us invariably precedes the terrible, awful and desolating hurricane. For twenty-five years European nations have been at peace with each other, and the several excitements that have created bloodshed, have been the civil commotions of individual nations. Twenty-five years of peace in Europe! The like has not occurred since Cæsar with his victorious legions invaded Britain near twenty centuries ago. This long spell of quiet and resting of armor have not arisen from any increase of peaceful morals, or love among nations. The lawyer's son of Corsica, that fiery symbol of despotic Democracy, had so drained Europe of her blood and her treasures, that the nations sympathetically, mechanically as it were, rested wearily upon their blood stained arms to recover once more their long spent strength. Napoleon, when at St. Helena, remarked that the next general war in Europe would end in a "war of opinion." This expression will be found prophetic.

There is not at this moment a nation in Europe but is prepared for war. England, in spite of her debt, and the miseries of a vast portion of her population, has increased her army; and her navy was never in a more fitting war condition than at the present time.

Steam, (as great an addition to modern war as gunpowder was of old,—and its mighty power is not yet fathomed,) England possesses in a degree, far superior to any other nation.

France contains probably the most powerful and effective army of any continental power. Her navy has rapidly increased and improved from former times, and, like England, her war steamers are numerous.

Prussia and Austria keep their armies organised on the war service, ready for immediate action.

Russia, the black bear of the north, with her hordes of invading Cossacks, and her countless thousands of serf soldiers, feared and hated by all Europe as much as the overwhelming Huns and Goths of old, stands ready to "let slip the dogs of war."

When the next conflict breaks out among any two of these five great nations, where will it end? God alone can determine. Is such a war far off? We think not—and our own country, perhaps, is destined to open the great political ball which will set the whole civilised world in the fiery course of a long and bloody war. Does it not, then, behove England to pause and contemplate her difficulties with us—her children, grown to manhood? Had she better not yield a little of that proud and haughty spirit, which through a thousand years of trimuphs and victories, has led her on to such a degree of ambition that she can bear no control in her desires and wishes? Her will has heretofore been her law. She should remember that Rome had its zenith; Greece reached her ascendancy and fell; Carthage was once the mistress of the seas; Troy has been, but is no more.

And *now* where are those once powerful and mighty nations—echo answers, where? They are remembered only in history, and the scholar of antiquity wanders among their classic ruins and reads in their remains the eternal revolving chapter of the decline and fall of empires.[2]

We put the question to any reflecting Englishman, what would most likely be the result of a contest between America and England. We are young and growing—the blows that we should feel would only be on the gristle, but to England the end would be disastrous, suicidal. The Canadas would be ours—other nations would be dragged into the way—England, possessing within herself the smothered fires of resistance, would become the victim of external aggression and intestine division, and she would fall like the avalanche, crushing away her public debt, her present form of government, her colonies, her church and her aristocracy in one general mine.

[APRIL 14, 1842]

LIFE AND LOVE[3]

Damps and chills continued—would have been a very good motto for yesterday. Five minutes to one P., M. we stood at the window, drumming idly on the pane with our fingers, and gazing at the magnificent prospect outside. Drizzle, drizzle, drizzle—drop, drop, drop —hour after hour, and no cessation. The omnibusses roll along, dragged by their melancholy horses; shivering pedestrians pass with a kind of dog trot on the side walks; and the old apple woman who generally occupies the corner over the way, is no where to be seen.

What a variety of umbrellas!

After gazing at the scene, and making divers philosophic speculations upon matters and things in general, we determined to perpetrate a few paragraphs of sentiment. Reader, get a fresh handkerchief.

Life and love! The words are certainly short, and make no great show in print; yet has each, in its four little letters, a mighty volume of mystery, and beauty. Were we disposed to be fanciful, we might divide the body's life from the mind's life, and compare them together. The first men share equally with irrational animals.

But the soul's life! The soul—so grand and noble in its capacities, so thirsty for knowledge, so filled with the germs of illimitable progress—the soul, that has such awful powers, is endued with such quickness, such judgment, such ability of thinking strange and unearthly thoughts, such a desire of assimilating itself to perfection and godlike purity, such insatiable anxiousness to discover hidden things, such unfathomable good will for its fellows, such undying faith in the efficiency of truth, and such towering ambition, that it may well be lost in wonder at itself. O, what venturesome mariner shall launch forth, and explore it, and take a plummet in his hand and sound its depths?

And part of the life of the soul is *love;* for the chambers of the heart are pleasant as well as costly. Things of surpassing fairness are there—thoughts that glow and dazzle—benevolence—innocent and holy friendship. Among their windings, restless and sparkling like rays of sunshine, lurk a hundred promptings and capabilities for delight. They are planted by God—and he who would stifle them is a bigot and a fool.

Ever faithful, too, there is the monitor conscience, sitting on her throne, with a sleepless eye, and a never tiring finger. And down, deep down, from the innermost recesses, wells up the pure fountain of affection, the sweetest and the most cheering of the heart's treasures.

What a superb verse that is of Coleridge's:

> "All thoughts, all passions, all delights—
> Whatever stirs this mortal frame,
> Are but the ministers of *love,*
> And feed his sacred flame."4

So let us be more just to our own nature, and to the gifts which the Almighty has made ineradicable within us. Casting our eyes over this beautiful earth, where so much of joy and sunshine exist —looking on the human race with the gentle orbs of kindness and philosophy—sending our glance through the cool and verdant lanes, by the sides of the blue rivers, over the crowded city, or among those who dwell on the prairies, or along the green savannahs of the south —and we shall see that everywhere are the seeds of *happiness* and *love.* Yet unless they are fostered, they will lie entombed forever in the darkness and their possessors may die and be buried, and never think of them but as baubles and worth no care.

[APRIL 20, 1842]

THE OCEAN

It is not easy for a person who has resided only upon the seaboard, to conceive of the feelings which fill the bosom of one, when for the first time he comes in sight of the ocean. How many thousands pass their lives without one glimpse of that glorious "creature," which, next to the canopy above, is the most magnificent object of material creation.

Here is one who has spent the years of childhood, youth, and early manhood in the far off inland districts. The green hills, briar studded crags, and mossy battlements of rock, have echoed with the bellowing of the thunder and the mountain blast, but with the deep, rolling murmur of the ocean, never. He has seen the flowers of the glen nod, and the treetops of the forest wave in the wind, and when the fury of the tempest came, the air filled with mangled branches and stripped off verdure; but never has he seen the ocean "wrought up to madness by the storm," the angry billows leaping up, and in battle array invading the province of the very clouds, or dashing in spent fury upon the trembling rocks. Calmly has he seen the moon throw down her light upon the rural bound, and all things revelling in quiet beauty; but never the moonlight rocked upon the rolling deep, nor the reflected stars rising and falling there, gems upon a mighty bosom swelling with darkness and mystery. Over wide spread fields of green, dotted with copse and mansion, has his eye wandered; but never over a boundless field of brightest blue, variegated only by the sunny sail and sable hull. What, then, can we imagine to be his feelings, as he stands now for the first time upon some lofty sea shore crag, with the boundless expanse before him? His soul must be stirred by its magnificence, and his thoughts take a new and loftier flight into regions of beauty and grandeur.

A few days ago we were quietly treading our way among the bales, boxes and crates upon one of the East river quays, when our progress was arrested by a very aged man, who wished to have pointed out to him the different kinds of vessels. He said he had never before seen vessels of any kind, this being the first time he had ever been near the ocean. He had read of the various classes, but had no definite conception on the subject. At first we thought him quizzing, but after being satisfied of his perfect sincerity, endeavored to point out the peculiarities. He soon had no difficulty in recognizing the various denominations—ships, barks, brigs, schooners, sloops, &c.; and as well as our limited nautical attainments would admit of, we endeavored to show the peculiar advantages of the different modes of rigging. The old man seemed much gratified, and doubtless will with pleasure, should it ever be our lot to peregrinate in the region of his home, point out to us the peculiarities, virtues, beauties and uses of the various productions of his soil. And that practical knowledge of his is of far greater value than all the fanciful smattering that is usually caught up in the city rounds. A man cannot acquire all knowledge, and therefore it becomes him to direct his attention to the acquisition of that which is of the greatest worth. Teaching a bean to wind up its pole, is a more useful, though perhaps not so *manly* or elegant an employment, as teaching a lap dog to jump.

But we were speaking of the ocean—that eternal fountain of the sublime and mysterious. We love to listen to the deep aud ceaseless tones of its music, when the repose of midnight has fallen upon it. There is a sublimity in its angry tossing, when wrought to madness by the assaults and goadings of the storm king. We love to think of the riches, and the lost, that lie beneath its wave, and to carry the thoughts forward to that eventful hour when it must give up its treasures and its dead—when the sands which now form its bound will melt away with "the fervent heat," and its waves be lost in the ocean of eternity.

[APRIL 21, 1842]

DREAMS

Dreams, to the pure of heart, are always messengers of love and beauty; be he the son of wealth or of poverty, they are to him a gilding which serves to adorn and beautify the roughest deformities of life. There are dreams of the day and dreams of the night, but around all fancy twines a magic wreath. Here is a mother watching her tender babe. What dreams must fill her anxious heart. By night, while on her breast that sweet one calmly breathes, and timid sleep has gently closed her eyes, she dreams of nought but beauty, love, and tenderness. By day she dreams of the proud moments when those pure lips will lisp the name of "mother"; then, when by her side it ambles to the fields, to revel with the flowers, and join its laugh with the gay robin's song; then to the school she follows it; and then to the distant and more sombre path beset by manhood's cares and duties, where she sees him, by his acts of honor and of virtue, shedding lustre on the name she gave; and then, in "melancholy pleasure," she dreamily reverts to the hour when old age will throw down his frosts upon her head, and find him by her side, a watchful one, who will support her tottering step, and smooth the pillow for her dying head. Sweet are the mother's dreams.

And here is the toiling aspirant for wealth. We let him pass. His dreams are sordid, unsatisfying, and unworthy of the form he bears. By day, his thoughts are running among boxes, bales, and tierces; notes, and bills, and bullion; ships, and lands, and houses;—and by night, the order only is reversed—they are running in his thoughts. Anxious and unsatisfying are the worldling's dreams.

And here is the blooming maiden. Her day dreams rest on fair and bright, though evanescent joys. The present is a sparkling holiday—the future, a sealed book, which she seldom urges fancy to step forward and unfold. And when her day of little cares has passed, and her quelled spirit seeks repose upon her virgin couch, visions of purity and peace hover around her head. Fair are the dreams of joyous maidenhood.

And here is the poor poet, with ashy cheek, but his eye whose power discovers beauty in the smallest thing of earth. Night's shadows fall, and his limbs, wearied with wandering, are stretched upon his coarse pallet; the gnawing pangs of appetite are eased by dreams of present love and future glory. Now he revels in the fields of brightness spread around, and anon tosses in nervous anticipation of that triumphant hour, when, on the glittering wings of genius he will soar to regions of such surpassing lustre as will dazzle all beholders, and far overpay his own physical toil and suffering. And from the waking dream he gently passes into that more glowing, less alloyed, one of sleep. Far brighter scenes than even he had viewed in waking hours, now crowd around his path; and even while they change and flit his newly opened vision, deems them enduring. But fleeting is that hour of immaterial radiance, and he wakes again to find himself upon the couch of poverty.

But yet his spirit sinks not. Poor though he be in worldly wealth, he has a soul which in Nature's volume reads a lesson which imparts content, nay, highest happiness. That is a holy volume, filled with the most true and glorious illustrations which the universe affords, and is opened wide to all—as well as to the meanest beggar as the mightiest lord—and he to whom God gave the soul to comprehend it, and to love its varied pages, is the happiest of his race, though poorest in the eye of undiscerning fools. And he who never drew life from that pure fountain, is poorest of the earth worm race, though bathing in a fount of gold. And this poor poet rises from his dreaming couch, to walk a dreaming path; and if but a crust of bread and a cup of water are his to stay the stern demands of hunger, he casts his eye upon morn's mantling blushes, the retreating mists, and opening flowers, and is well satisfied. Finally, as life progresses, he finds that one by one his earlier dreams — that all his earthborn dreams—are fading into nothingness; and as his mind has long been drawn from earth's corroding cares and gold increasing toils, he wakes—aye, *wakes* to revel in the glories of that world beyond the veil.

And there are children's dreams—fair, but transient. They come, like the zephyr, to impart warmth and cheer to the tender spirit. By night, like little stars, they twinkle through the mists of undeveloped intellect, and by day throw a veil of undefined beauty over the play ground and the fair scenes of home.

[APRIL 23, 1842]

TIME TO COME[5]

By Walter Whitman

O, Death! a black and pierceless pall
  Hangs round thee, and the future state;
No eye may see, no mind may grasp
  That mystery of Fate.

This brain, which now alternate throbs
  With swelling hope and gloomy fear;
This heart, with all the changing hues,
  That mortal passions bear—

This curious frame of human mould,
  Where unrequited cravings play,
This brain, and heart, and wondrous form
  Must all alike decay.

The leaping blood will stop its flow;
  The hoarse death-struggle pass; the cheek
Lay bloomless, and the liquid tongue
  Will then forget to speak.

The grave will tame me; earth will close
  O'er cold dull limbs and ashy face;
But where, O, Nature, where shall be
  The soul's abiding place?

Will it e'en live? for though its light
  Must shine till from the body torn;
Then, when the oil of life is spent,
  Still shall the taper burn?

O, powerless is this struggling brain
  To rend the mighty mystery;
In dark, uncertain awe it waits
  The common doom, to die.

[APRIL 9, 1842]

THE DEATH AND BURIAL OF McDONALD CLARKE.
A PARODY.[6]

Not a sign was heard, not a tear was shed,
  As away to the "tombs"[7] he was hurried,
No mother or friend held his dying head,
  Or wept when the poet was buried.

They buried him lonely; no friend stood near,
  (The scoffs of the multitude spurning,)
To weep o'er the poet's sacred bier;
  No bosom with anguish was burning.

No polish'd coffin enclosed his breast,
  Nor in purple or linen they wound him,
As a stranger he died; he went to his rest
  With cold charity's shroud wrapt 'round him.

Few and cold were the prayers they said,
  Cold and dry was the cheek of sadness,
Not a tear of grief baptised his head,
  Nor of sympathy pardon'd his madness.

None thought, as they stood by his lowly bed,
  Of the griefs and pains that craz'd him;
None thought of the sorrow that turn'd his head,
  Of the vileness of those who prais'd him.

Lightly they speak of his anguish and woe,
  And o'er his cold ashes upbraid him,
By whatever he was that was evil below,
  Unkindness and *cruelty made* him.

Ye hypocrites! stain not his grave with a tear,
  Nor blast the fresh planted willow
That weeps o'er his grave; for while he was here,
  Ye refused him a crumb and a pillow.

Darkly and sadly his spirit has fled,
  But his name will long linger in story;
He needs not a stone to hallow his bed;
  He's in Heaven, encircled with glory.

[MARCH 18, 1842]   [Signed]   W.

ℐlotes

Preface

1. For an account of the discovery, see Joseph Jay Rubin, "Whitman's New York Aurora," *American Literature*, (1939), pp. 214-217.

Introduction

1. Thomas Low Nichols, *Forty Years of American Life, 1821-1861* (New York: Stackpole Sons, 1937), p. 167.
2. *Aurora*, Feb. 5, 1842.
3. The quotation is from *Hamlet*, act III, sc. 2, l. 165.:

> And crook the pregnant hinges of the knee
> Where thrift may follow fawning.

4. Walt Whitman, *Complete Prose Works* (New York: D. Appleton and Co., 1910), p. 188. The other "Walks in Broadway" appeared Feb. 24, 25, and 26 and March 1 and 4.
5. *Aurora*, April 9, 1842.
6. Brooklyn *Eagle*, March 30, 1842.
7. *Aurora*, March 30, 1842.
8. *Ibid.*, April 6, 1842.
9. *Idem.*
10. *Aurora*, March 30, 1842.
11. *Ibid.*, March 30, 1842.
12. *Ibid.*, April 13, 1842.
13. *Ibid.*, April 14, 1842.
14. *Ibid.*, March 30, 1842.
15. *Ibid.*, April 7, 1842.
16. *Ibid.*, March 30, 1842.
17. *Ibid.*, March 8, 1842.
18. *Ibid.*, April 7, 1842.
19. *Ibid.*, April 16, 1842.
20. *Ibid.*, April 6, 1842.
21. *Ibid.*, March 14, 1842.
22. *Ibid.*, April 28, 1842.
23. *Ibid.*, March 29, 1842.
24. *Ibid.*, March 22, 1842.
25. *Ibid.*, April 20, 1842.
26. Horace Traubel, *With Walt Whitman in Camden* (Vol. I, Boston: Small, Maynard and Co., 1906. Vol. II, New York: D. Appleton and Co., 1908. Vol. III, New York: Mitchell Kennerly, 1914), II, pp. 25-26.
27. *Aurora*, April 7, 1842.
28. *The Conservator*, XII, (1901), p. 76.

Part One

1. Whitman may have used this article and the one following as the basis for a sketch published under the title of "Broadway" in *Life Illustrated*, Aug. 9, 1856. The organization, phraseology, and details are very similar. See *New York Dissected*, ed. by Emory Holloway and Ralph Adimari (New York: Rufus Rockwell Wilson, Inc., 1936), pp. 119-124.

2. The *Aurora* office was at 162 Nassau Street. The area later became known as "Printing-House Square," because nearly all the Democratic papers were published in the vicinity of Tammany Hall.

3. A "Grahamite" was a follower of Sylvester Graham, the food reformer who advocated a diet of whole wheat bread, coarse cereals, vegetables, and fresh fruits.

4. Whitman wrote in "Song of Myself," ll. 209-210:

> *The butcher-boy puts off his killing clothes,*
> *or sharpens his knife at the stall in the*
> *market:*
> *I loiter and enjoy his repartee, and his shuffle*
> *and breakdown.*

5. In writing this article, Whitman was on familiar grounds. Since his early teens, he had "boarded out," as he was to do most of his life until he finally made his home on Mickle Street in Camden, New Jersey. In an article which he is supposed to have written about himself for the *Critic* in 1885, he stated: "Quite a good deal of his life has been passed in boarding houses and hotels." See *The Uncollected Poetry and Prose of Walt Whitman*, ed. by Emory Holloway (New York: Doubleday, Doran and Co., 1921), II, p. 59. Whitman also described the grades of New York boarding houses in his temperance novel, *Franklin Evans*.

6. Frances Trollope in her *Domestic Manners of the Americans,* first published in 1832, expressed horror at the American male's habit of spitting. The habit also was disliked by Charles Dickens, who had arrived for a visit in this country just before Whitman became editor of the *Aurora*.

7. "Mrs. C—" is probably the Mrs. Chipman mentioned by Whitman in the following entry in a manuscript notebook: "Went to New York in May 1841 and wrote for *Democratic Review*, worked at printing business in *New World* office boarded at Mrs. Chipmans—." See *The Uncollected Poetry and Prose of Walt Whitman*. II, p. 87.

8. The theme of this tale—the fate of a profligate—and the name of the character are reminiscent of Whitman's story, "Wild Frank's Return," published in the *Democratic Review* in Nov., 1841. They are also suggestive of the main character in *Franklin Evans*.

9. Whitman later formed many friendships with bus drivers and, instead of finding their life dull, often rode with them on their trips.

10. Rappee is a dark, coarse, strong-flavored snuff.

11. The incidents in this article may have suggested some of the passages in *Franklin Evans*.

12. Grant Thorburn was a popular New York florist.

13. William Niblo was owner of a fashionable entertainment center at the northeast corner of Broadway and Prince Street. His place was known as Niblo's Gardens.

14. The Crosby Street synagogue was built in 1833.

15. These objects were the *torahs*.

16. Mordecai M. Noah, famous as a lawyer, playwright, and journalist, was at this time an associate judge of the New York Court of Sessions. He was appointed to the post by Governor William Henry Seward in 1841.

17. The Washingtonians were members of the popular temperance society.

18. Whitman held this same attitude later when he edited the Brooklyn *Eagle*. He wrote: "The Brooklyn *Eagle* wishes every body in general, and some persons in particular, to understand that it considers its presence at any public place—at *any* place, where it goes in its capacity as the *B. E.*—to be a *special favor*, a thing for the place and persons visited to show themselves thankful for, and to bless their stars for." See *The Gathering of the Forces*. ed. by Cleveland Rodgers and John Black (New York: G. P. Putnam's Sons, 1920) II, p. 342.

19. The *Washingtonian*, edited by James Burns, was established by the owners of the *Aurora* on March 19, 1842. It was published weekly. The *Aurora* frequently reprinted articles from the *Washingtonian*—a cheap way of filling up the paper, since the type did not have to be reset.

20. Whitman reprinted this article, with some minor changes, in the Brooklyn *Eagle* under the caption, "A City Fire," on Feb. 24, 1847. See *The Uncollected Poetry and Prose of Walt Whitman*. I, pp. 154-156.

21. A notice advertising a meeting to protest removal of the remains of persons buried in the Baptist cemetery at Delancey and Chrystie Streets appeared in the *Aurora* on March 12, 1842. The ground was to be taken over by the Hudson Fire Insurance Company and sold for house lots. On this date, Whitman wrote a short editorial asking if it were possible "that men will do such things for money." Another meeting was called for March 28, and Whitman returned to the subject in a second short editorial in which he protested: "Let not the almighty dollar so benumb our finer feelings, that we have no reverence for the bones of our buried fathers." The passions of the people were so inflamed that when workmen began digging into the graves on March 28 they and police called to protect them were routed by a crowd of a hundred or more men and women. An incident of this riot resulted in Whitman's editorial praising the woman who armed herself with a pistol to protect the graves of her dead ones.

22. This editorial is similar in thought and phraseology to one written by Whitman for the Brooklyn *Eagle* protesting the razing of Fort Greene Park. In the *Eagle* Whitman wrote other editorials condemning what he called "the morbid appetite for money." See *The Gathering of the Forces*, II, pp. 46-50, 130-136.

23. Fanny Kemble, a leading actress, was much admired by Whitman.

24. Bishop John Hughes organized the Catholics and the Irish immigrants in a campaign to secure state support for parochial schools. He was bitterly castigated by Whitman. See editorials in Part II.

25. The *Aurora* attacked Daniel Webster because of his alleged extramartial amours and loose living. These attacks were begun before Whitman joined the newspaper.

26. Justice Matsell, a police court magistrate, was assailed by Whitman following Matsell's action in having arrested about fifty prostitutes on Broadway. Whitman condemned the wholesale arrest in editorials on March 24, 25, 26, and 30, 1842. His longest editorial apparently appeared on March 25, but this issue of the *Aurora* is missing. The gist of this editorial was given on March 26 in a short article, as follows:

> *The language we used in our article of yesterday, denouncing*
> *the kidnapping of women in Broadway, by the police authorities,*
> *was not intended and does not apply to them as citizens. We*
> *meant only to say that the kidnapping and imprisoning of these*
> *women, on Wednesday night, was a ruffianly, scoundrelly, villain-*
> *ous, outrageous and high handed proceeding, unsanctioned by*
> *law, justice, humanity, virtue, or religion; and yet the justices and*
> *officers may be decent, upright, well meaning, and faithful in their*
> *duties as public servants and as citizens. The whole proceeding*
> *was villainous—wrong—but perhaps we may have used rather*
> *hard words in denouncing it.*

Whitman discussed the problem of prostitution and the sex life of the un-
married boldly in the Brooklyn *Times;* the *Aurora* editorials indicate his early
thinking on the matter. See *I Sit and Look Out,* ed. by Emory Holloway and
Vernolian Schwarz (New York: Columbia University Press, 1932), pp. 111-122.

27. See note 7.

28. This self-portrait by Whitman corresponds to the picture of him
given by William Cauldwell, for many years editor of the New York *Mer-*
cury. Cauldwell, at the age of seventeen, worked as an apprentice printer in
the *Aurora* shop. He wrote of Whitman in a letter to the New York *Times*
(reprinted in the *Conservator,* XII, No. 5, July 1901, p. 76):

> *Mr. Whitman was at that time, I should think, about 25 years*
> *of age, tall and graceful in appearance, neat in attire, and pos-*
> *sessed a very pleasing and impressive eye and a cheerful, happy-*
> *looking countenance. He usually wore a frock coat and high hat,*
> *carried a small cane, and the lapel of his coat was almost invari-*
> *ably ornamented with a boutonniere . . .*

> *Mr. Whitman, for some reason, took a fancy to me, and al-*
> *ways accorded me a cheery greeting, and, notwithstanding the*
> *difference in our ages, we became quite chummy. Frequently,*
> *while I was engaged in sticking type, he would ask me to let him*
> *take my case for a little while, and he seemed to enjoy the rec-*
> *reation . . .*

> *After he looked over the daily and exchange papers (reach-*
> *ing the den he occupied usually between 11 and 12 o'clock), it*
> *was Mr. Whitman's daily habit to stroll down Broadway to the*
> *Battery, spending an hour or two amid the trees and enjoying the*
> *water view, returning to the office location at about 2 or 3 o'clock*
> *in the afternoon . . .*

29. Park Benjamin, editor, poet, dramatist, was often attacked in the
Aurora. See Part IV.

30. The figure was meant to represent Park Benjamin.

31. Charles Dickens.

32. Whitman mentions the custom in almost the same words in one of
his "Sun-Down Papers" published in the *Long Island Democrat* on Aug. 11,
1840, and in a story, "The Little Sleighers," printed in the *Columbian Maga-*
zine in Sept. 1844. See *The Uncollected Poetry and Prose of Walt Whitman,*
I, pp. 35-37, 90-92.

33. This may be a disguised reference to Edward, Whiman's youngest
brother, who was always mentally a child. Whitman was very fond of Edward,
but he worried about him constantly all his life.

34. When Whitman was in Jamaica two years before, he lived near the famous Union race track. On May 10, 1842—the most exciting day Jamaica had experienced since the race in 1823 between Henry and Eclipse—Fashion ran against Boston for a purse of $20,000.

Part Two

1. With this editorial, the *Aurora* violently launched its attack against the efforts of Bishop John Hughes to get part of the city's public school money allocated to parochial schools. In the salutatory editorial of the first issue on Nov. 24, 1841, the *Aurora* owners announced that their new paper would be an "American" publication, charging that most of the other papers were operated by "foreigners." But until the public school question was made a political issue by Bishop Hughes, the *Aurora* had not been especially "Nativist" in its sympathies, and it had printed only one attack against the Catholics before this date. The riot described by Whitman in this editorial seems to have been the provocation which led to his series of denunciatory editorials.

2. This meeting was called by a group of citizens to protest a measure before the state legislature at Albany to set up a new system of school administration designed primarily to permit the Catholics to share in the public fund for their parochial schools. Under the supervision of the city council, the school funds at the time were managed by the Public School Society. The city council banned the allocation of money to any sectarian school or any school in which religion was taught. Two years before, in 1840, Governor William H. Seward had recommended in his message to the legislature "the establishment of schools in which [the children of New York] may be instructed by teachers speaking the same language with themselves and professing the same faith." He said that many children were denied the opportunity of education because of religious and racial bias. The governor's recommendations to alter the school system were included in a measure introduced in the legislature by William B. Maclay, which was up for consideration when Whitman joined the *Aurora*. Thus the long-simmering controversy came to a boil during his editorship. This fact helps to explain the especial virulence of his editorials.

3. This probably was Josiah Rich, former alderman, who offered the set of resolutions opposing the Maclay bill. He excused himself from reading them because of "feebleness of voice," according to the *Aurora* account, and the long resolutions were then read by Thomas Fessenden "in a loud and distinct tone."

4. Bishop John Hughes was born in County Tyrone, Ireland, Jan. 24, 1797. He came to the United States in 1817, a year after his parents emigrated to America. After training for the priesthood, he held pastorates in Bedford, Pa., and Philadelphia before going to St. Mary's Church in New York City. An ambitious man, he became influential not only within the church but outside it as well. He engaged in a strong defense of the Catholics in the early years of the Nativist movement. He was consecrated titular bishop of Basileopolis on Jan. 7, 1838, but was not to succeed the formal command until Dec. 20, 1842. Evidently not a person to serve in a secondary position, he immediately gained control of the diocese. His stormy career was ended by his death on Jan. 3, 1864.

5. The Spartan Band was composed of young Tammany Democrats of the sixth ward, led by Michael Walsh. It later figured in election-day riots

described in subsequent editorials. Walsh, a self-educated laborer, worked a few weeks as a reporter on the *Aurora* after Whitman left the paper. Walsh became a stormy petrel in New York machine politics; he later served as alderman and was elected to a term in Congress.

6. The *New Era* was a Tammany organ, edited by Levi D. Slamm. His "sledge-hammer" journalism and politics caused him to be referred to as "Slamm, Bang & Co." by James Gordon Bennett in the New York *Herald*.

7. For comments by Whitman on these papers see the editorial, "The New York Press" in Part IV.

8. Robert H. Morris was then mayor and a candidate for renomination for the forthcoming April election. Whitman approved of him, because he opposed religious or sectarian teaching in the public schools.

9. This, of course, is an open bid by the *Aurora* to be designated the official Tammany organ. The *Aurora* from its first issue had maintained that it was not a partisan newspaper, largely because it had not been given the support of any party. It later became a strongly pro-Tyler paper.

10. This editorial is important for its explanation of Whitman's violent expressions against the Catholics and the Irish and German immigrants. It should to some extent clear him of accusations of narrow bigotry. A Jeffersonian democrat, he strongly believed in separation of church and state—a principle which would be violated if sectarian schools received public money. He also opposed a "religious" party, toward which Bishop Hughes' organization of the Catholic voters tended. Similar beliefs are expressed in the last editorial in this section "[Native Americanism Repudiated]." His opposition to foreign influences of course was commonplace in that period, conforming to such respectable manifestoes as Emerson's "The American Scholar," delivered in 1837. Whitman at this time was an admirer of the notorious reformer, Frances Wright, who opposed religious teaching in the schools.

11. David Dudley Field, later a noted lawyer, was a Democratic candidate for the New York Assembly in 1841.

12. Aaron J. Vanderpoel, a lawyer.

13. Robert Sedgwick, Field's law partner.

14. John Morrell, a lawyer.

15. The Hughes-supported candidate was Thomas O'Connor, nominated as an "Independent Democratic Republican."

16. The lines are from *Macbeth*, Act III, sc. 1, l. 71.

17. Isaac L. Varian, Democratic senator and former New York mayor. He was elected to the legislature by the Tammany organization in 1839 and 1840.

18. Judge Scott was also a Democratic senator.

19. The *Arena* was edited by Thomas Low Nichols, Whitman's predecessor on the *Aurora*.

20. Although he professed to be a Democrat, Whitman during his newspaper career was frequently at odds with the party. While editing the Brooklyn *Eagle* in 1848, he broke with the regular Democratic party over the slavery question, joining the radical Democrats in supporting the Free-Soil party. When he joined the Brooklyn *Times* in 1857 (his last regular newspaper connection), Whitman had learned the lesson that partisan journalism was not for him and had given up the hope that he could adhere to any party organization.

21. Colonel Alexander Hamilton, who also had presided at the meeting on April 8 at which James Monroe was nominated as the "Tyler candidate" for mayor.

22. J. Phillips Phoenix was the Whig candidate for mayor.
23. Robert W. Morris was the Democratic candidate for re-election as mayor.
24. Aaron J. Vanderpoel, born at Kinderhook, New York.
25. A popular medicament advertised in the *Aurora* as a cure for consumption, colds, coughs, asthma, worms, headaches and palpitations, weak backs, corns, and sundry other human afflictions.
26. These were Spartans, the group of Tammany Democrats headed by Michael Walsh.
27. Whitman's profession of having obtained the "authentic" details for this article is not exactly honest. William Cullen Bryant's *Evening Post*, which had counseled conciliation and restraint in the school controversy, in an article on April 13, said that the election riots started in the sixth ward when a group of Spartans upset ballot boxes in which Whig votes were kept. Then the band went to the eleventh, thirteenth, and seventh wards. The Irish armed themselves and paraded up and down to defend the polls. When they encountered the Spartans, fights resulted, especially at the Sixth Ward Hotel. The *Post* blamed the riots on "the inflammatory appeals which have lately been addressed to vulgar prejudices from certain presses and pulpits." Besides the *Aurora*, the *Herald*, James Gordon Bennett's paper, and the *Commercial Advertiser*, published by W. L. Stone, were accused by Bishop Hughes of being instigators of the rioting mobs.

Part Three

1. Richard III, act V, sc. 3, l. 12. The original reads: "Which they of the adverse party want."
2. Clay was nominated by the Whigs at Harrisburg in 1844.
3. The manifesto was a thirteen-page letter, written in Oct. 1841, in which Scott described himself as an "old-fashioned republican devoted to the support of law and order—a democratic Whig."
4. See the editorial on Calhoun printed March 24, 1842.
5. The *Aurora*, some time after Whitman quit as editor, became a pro-Tyler paper.
6. John Tyler.
7. While Whitman may be pretending in this editorial to a knowledge and experience he did not possess, his reference to Webster in the campaign of 1840 is based on fact. Whitman was working on the *Long Island Democrat* in Jamaica, when Webster spoke there Sept. 24, 1840, in behalf of William Henry Harrison. An ardent young Democrat, Whitman took the political stump to refute Webster's speech.
8. The ideas expressed in this article were a part of Whitman's general theory of democracy, and were repeated frequently in his writings.
9. Whitman gained his first real literary recognition through his contributions to the *Democratic Review* in 1841 and 1842. It was one of the nation's leading magazines, publishing work by such writers as Bryant, Lowell, Whittier, Longfellow, Paulding, and Simms.
10. Whitman expressed similar sentiments in an editorial in the Brooklyn *Eagle* on May 14, 1846. See *The Gathering of the Forces*, ed. by Cleveland Rodgers and John Black (New York: G. P. Putnam's Sons, 1920), II, pp. 191-192.

11.   March 11, "How Bears the Wind?"

12.   William Henry Harrison.

13.   John Tyler.

14.   Whitman's fondness for French phrases usually is attributed to his three months spent in New Orleans working on the *Crescent*. His *Aurora* writings indicate that he fancied them even before going to New Orleans. The accounts of balls and soirees contributed voluminously to the *Aurora* by penny-a-liners, were liberally sprinkled with fashionable French phrases, and Whitman could easily have formed the habit of using them.

15.   Whitman was a life-long opponent to the protective tariff.

16.   Whitman reprinted parts of this editorial in an article, "You Cannot Legislate Men into Virtue," in the Brooklyn *Eagle*, March 18, 1846. See *The Gathering of the Forces*, I pp. 59-61.

Part Four

1.   This was one of Emerson's series of lectures on "The Times." The adresses included "The Times," March 3; "The Poet," March 5; "The Conservative," March 7; "The Transcendentalist," March 9; "Manners," March 12; and "Prospects," March 14. Whitman later mentioned hearing Bryant and Emerson lecture in the halls of the Athenaeum and Historical Societies on Broadway, but gave no dates. Perhaps he may have had in mind Emerson's 1842 addresses. See *Complete Prose Works* (New York: D. Appleton and Co., 1910), p. 518.

2.   Full reports of all of Emerson's lectures on "The Times," running to a column in length, were published by Horace Greeley in the *Tribune*.

3.   Whitman reprinted most of this article in the Brooklyn *Eagle* on June 13, 1846, under the heading, "An Afternoon at Greenwood." Clarke was buried in Greenwood Cemetery on Long Island. See *The Gathering of the Forces*, ed. by Cleveland Rodgers and John Black (New York: G. P. Putnam's Sons, 1910), II, pp. 105-113.

McDonald Clarke, known as "the mad poet," was a familiar Broadway figure. Clarke was born in Bath, Maine, June 18, 1798. He lived in direst poverty in New York from 1819 until his death. His sole income was from the sale of his poems to newspapers, but he was aided by his friends, including Fitz-Green Halleck, who wrote a poem about him. He was often ridiculed for his eccentricities, and his final break over into insanity was supposed to have been caused by a practical joke played upon him: some person had deceived him by promising to introduce him to a woman whose beauty had attracted him.

Thomas Low Nichols, Whitman's predecessor on the *Aurora*, was among those who befriended Clarke. On Dec. 24, 1841, Nichols wrote that all Clarke "needs is a good editor, to be immortalized." Perhaps Nichols thought he was that editor, for in January and February he published twelve of Clarke's poems.

Clarke's last poems sent to the *Aurora* were signed "Afara." Nichols described an encounter with Clarke on Christmas night, 1842, in which the poet, babbling incoherently, said that he was dead, his brains having been smashed out at the foot of the monument of Thomas A. Emmett in St. Paul's churchyard. A part of Clarke's fantasy was that he had become "Afara, an Archangel of the Almighty." The poems sent to the *Aurora*, Nichols wrote, were "insane" in "chirography," "difficult to unravel as a skein of tangled gold." Clarke died March 5, about the time Whitman started writing for the *Aurora.*

4. Considering Whitman's youthful passion for the drama and the opera, surprisingly little is found in the *Aurora* to indicate his interests and apprecia- tions. The *Aurora* carried short notices of a hundred words or so of the per- formances at the Chatham, Olympic, Bowery, and Park theatres, mentioning merely the names of the play or opera, the performers, and perhaps the recep- tion of them by the audience. The scarcity of musical and dramatic criticism may be due to the fact that Whitman had other editorial duties. Employment on a morning newspaper naturally meant that his presence was required in the office when he might have preferred participating in the night-time diversions of the city.

5. All the actors mentioned by Whitman in this editorial—Thomas Barry, Miss Buloid, Susan Cushman, Mrs. C. Pritchard, Mrs. E. Knight, Henry Placide, John Fisher, and W. H. Williams—were well known and popular. The drama presented at the Park was generally of a higher quality than that given in other theatres.

6. Although almost unremembered today, Park Benjamin was one of the best known professional literary men of the mid-nineteenth century. He was frequently attacked in the *Aurora* even before Whitman joined the paper. Benjamin went to New York in 1838, after having edited for a time the *New England Magazine* in Boston. For a short time he was literary editor of Horace Greeley's *New Yorker;* then he had a brief connection with the *Evening Tattler* (edited by Whitman after leaving the *Aurora)* and the *Brother Jonathan,* a literary weekly. In 1839 he founded the *New World,* which throve by pirating popular British fiction. Since Whitman worked for the *New World* in May, 1841, as a printer, he may have had a personal grudge against Benjamin. Benjamin usually quarreled, sooner rather than later, with his associates; and he was, in all his editorial work, noted for his personal abuse of other editors and prominent literary figures.

7. The *New World* was one of the papers with offices on Ann Street. Other papers on this "newspaper row" were the *Herald, Tribune,* and *Planet.* The *Aurora* frequently referred to them as "the Ann street press."

8. The comedy was "The Fiscal Agent," produced Feb. 28, 1842. It failed after the third night.

9. Abner Kneeland was for a time a Universalist clergyman. He later became a well known agnostic, heading the First Society of Free Enquirers in Boston. He was imprisoned for blasphemy in articles printed in his publication, the *Boston Investigator.*

10. Frances Wright, a noted reformer and free thinker, was much ad- mired by Whitman. He espoused many of the doctrines she preached.

11. Benjamin was born in Demerara, British Guiana, the son of a Yankee sea captain. His mother was a native of the Barbadoes. He had lived in the United States since the age of four.

12. The first successful penny paper in New York was Benjamin Day's the *Sun.* It was immensely popular, read by mechanics, workmen, and the poorer classes. Its popular and financial success led to the establishment of many other "cheap papers." By 1842, many of the so called "penny" papers sold for two cents. The older commercial papers were much larger in size and sold for six cents.

13. For example, President Tyler designated James Gordon Bennett, publisher of the New York *Herald,* as the official printer for the southern New York district. The appointment was greeted by the *Aurora* with almost a col-

umn-long diatribe against Bennett, headed: "Outrage upon the American People—the President and His New Appointed Pimp."

14. According to Frederic Hudson in *Journalism in the United States, from 1690 to 1872* (New York: Harper and Bros., 1873), there were in New York in 1842 nine penny and twopenny papers, seven sixpenny papers, six Saturday papers, and five Sunday papers. No accurate count actually could be made, as Whitman pointed out, because new papers were constantly being started and others were as constantly being discontinued.

15. The *Evening Post,* edited by William Cullen Bryant since 1829, was one of the most respected papers, liberal in tone but nevertheless well balanced and "refined" in a period of scurrilous journalism. Whitman throughout his entire life esteemed Bryant as a poet.

16. The *Commercial Advertiser* had been edited since 1821 by Colonel William L. Stone. Its contributors included some excellent writers, and Stone himself was praised as a writer of tales and history.

17. The *American* was edited by Charles King, who assumed the position in 1823. He was a scholarly man and a finished writer, but lacked news enterprise. His paper merged in 1845 with the *Courier and Enquirer.*

18. The *Journal of Commerce* was published by Gerard Hallock and David Hale, both men of strong religious scruples and independence in character. They were among the most enterprising newsgatherers in New York.

19. The *Express* was founded in 1836 by James and Erastus Brooks. The brothers would go to great expense to get the news, once chartering a Hudson River steamer to bring election returns from Albany to New York.

20. The *Courier and Enquirer* editor was pugnacious James Watson Webb, quick to challenge to a duel or to cane an enemy. He twice attacked James Gordon Bennett on the street.

21. The *Tribune* was founded by Horace Greeley on April 10, 1841, a few months before the establishment of the *Aurora.* Greeley had built up a circulation of about 10,000 in a year's time, and his paper's circulation was surpassed only by the *Sun* and the *Herald.* Greeley was a Whig.

22. The *Sun,* then published by Moses Y. Beach, still had the largest circulation of any paper in New York. The first of the penny papers and an exploiter of lively news, the *Sun* was the best known sheet in the country.

23. The *Standard,* published by John M. Mumford, in 1842 was almost ready to expire. Hudson gave it a circulation of only 400.

24. James Gordon Bennett's *Herald* was the *bete noire* of the *Aurora,* as well as other papers. The *Aurora* hardly let a day pass without an editorial or squib lambasting Bennett.

25. The *New Era,* established in 1836 by Jared W. Bell, was the official Tammany organ, and Bell was the official printer for the city.

26. This theme, minus the attack on James Gordon Bennett, was developed somewhat earlier by Whitman in an article, "Boz and Democracy," published in the *Brother Jonathan,* Feb. 26, 1842. See *The Uncollected Poetry and prose of Walt Whitman,* ed. by Emory Holloway (Garden City, N. Y.: Doubleday, Page and Co., 1921), I, pp. 67-72.

27. Bennett was born in Scotland.

28. Hudson gave the *Aurora's* circulation as 5,000. Penny papers with greater circulations were the *Sun, Herald,* and *Tribune.* Several of the sixpenny sheets also had larger circulations than the *Aurora.*

29. The lines are from the *Odyssey,* bk. III, l, 621:

> *But when Aurora, daughter of the dawn,*
> *With rosy lustre purpled o'er the lawn.*

30. By Vincenzo Bellini. It was sung several times at the Park during April in a translation by J. R. Fry.

31. Euphrasia Borghese, an operatic soprano.

32. The persons mentioned by Whitman were all popular singers or actors.

33. Between the years 1837 and 1845, Cooper brought fourteen civil libel suits and instigated two criminal libel prosecutions against newspaper editors, charging publication of malicious falsehoods

Part Five

1. This is the only *Aurora* editorial by Whitman that mentions slavery or abolition.

2. This echoes Volney's *Ruins*, one of Whitman's favorite works.

3. Whitman contributed a story with a closely similar title, "A Legend of Life and Love," to the July, 1842, issue of the *Democratic Review*. The editorial's sentiments are also those of one of Whitman's Sun-Down Papers, published in the *Long Island Democrat,* July 6, 1841. See *The Uncollected Poetry and Prose of Walt Whitman*, ed. by Emory Holloway (New York: Doubleday, Doran and Co., 1921) I, pp. 46-48, 78-83.

4. The stanza is from Coleridge's "Love."

5. This poem is a revised version of an earlier poem titled "Our Future Lot," published in the *Long Islander,* a paper which Whitman owned and edited in 1838. It was printed by Emory Holloway in *The Uncollected Poetry and Prose of Walt Whitman* (I, pp.1-2) as the earliest example of Whitman's published verse. Holloway's version, however, was not copied from the *Long Islander* but from the *Long Island Democrat* of Oct. 31, 1838, which had picked it up from Whitman's paper. No issues of the *Long Islander* are known to exist. The *Long Island Democrat* version was not signed, and Holloway attributed the poem to Whitman on the assumption that he wrote all the material in the *Long Islander.* Whitman's publishing of "Time to Come" in the *Aurora* under his own signature verifies Holloway's assumption. The *Aurora* poem contains five revised stanzas of the eight in the earlier version and two entirely new stanzas, the first and the fourth.

6. Whitman's "parody" is an imitation of the Rev. Charles Wolfe's currently popular "The Burial of Sir John Moore." The British soldier was killed during an attack on Corunna and was buried on the field "with his martial cloak around him." Whitman's imitation follows the original closely in meter and diction.

7. Clarke was taken to the Tombs, the New York prison, when he lost his mind in the two or three weeks before his death.

Index